T0266593

THE LITTLE BLUE BOOK OF
SAILING WISDOM

THE LITTLE BLUE BOOK OF
SAILING WISDOM

Edited by
Stephen Brennan

Skyhorse Publishing

Skyhorse Publishing books may be purchased in bulk at special
discounts for sales promotion, corporate gifts, fund-raising, or
educational purposes. Special editions can also be created to specifi-
cations. For details, contact the Special Sales Department, Skyhorse
Publishing, 307 West 36th Street, 11th Floor, New York, NY 10018 or
info@skyhorsepublishing.com.

Skyhorse® and Skyhorse Publishing® are registered trademarks of
Skyhorse Publishing, Inc.®, a Delaware corporation.

Visit our website at www.skyhorsepublishing.com.

10 9 8 7 6 5 4

Library of Congress Cataloging-in-Publication Data is available on file.

ISBN: 978-1-62873-762-2

Printed in China

Contents

Introduction   vii

Part One   The Deep Blue Sea   1
Part Two   Seamen and Women   27
Part Three   Ship   50
Part Four   Storm and Calm   82
Part Five   Weather-Eye   113
Part Six   The Philosophic Sailor   134
Part Seven   Sea-Fever   175
              Appendix   186
              A Sailor's Glossary   188
              Index   208

They that go down to the sea in ships, that do business in great waters;
These see the works of the LORD and his wonders in the deep.
For he commandeth and raiseth the stormy wind, which lifteth up the waves thereof,
They mount up to the heavens, they go down into the depths; their soul is melted because of trouble.
They reel to and fro, and stagger like a drunken man, and are at their wits' end.
They cry unto the LORD in their trouble, and he bringeth them out of their distresses.
He maketh the storm a calm, so that the waves thereof are still.
Then they are glad because they be quiet; so he bringeth them into their desired haven.

Psalm 107: 23-30 AV

INTRODUCTION

When your life feels too difficult to rise above,
Sail away, sail away.

—NOEL COWARD

W hich one of us has not dreamed of this? We put away our troubles and run away to sea and lose ourselves in a life of daring and adventure. Without doubt, sailing is *the great escape.* We "turn our backs on the land," as the poet says, and all that that implies; because when you take yourself to sea, you leave behind, at least for a time, all the mundane, humdrum imperatives of your day-to-day breathing in and out. You skip out on all your difficulties, shattered friendships, bad debts, and broken hearts. To sail away is to flee, certainly, but it also may be best understood as a flight *to* something. Because the sailor aims to make a new start, to breath free air, to skin his eyes afresh on impossible vistas, to test himself upon a hostile, or at any rate foreign, element and match wits, skill, and luck with all the gods of the sea.

In all our literature, writings about the sea may be said to be the best pedigree. Just consider the authorial DNA here on offer: Joseph Conrad, Ernest Hemingway, Henry Thoreau, Jack

Kerouac, William Shakespeare, Samuel Johnson, and Sterling Hayden; the poets: John Masefield, Samuel Taylor Coleridge, Walt Whitman, Alfred Tennyson, and Gerard Manley Hopkins; the single-handers and explorers: Francis Chichester, Joshua Slocum, Tristan Jones, and Sir Francis Drake; and many more. A number of our founding epics also feature sea lit; Homer's *Odyssey* may be said to be a tale of the wanderings of a sailing man, and even the *Holy Bible* is shot through with sailing stories. But my own guilty secret is that I love the aphorisms best that concern the *how-to's* of ship-handling, sailing, and sea-lore.

There are some people the sea does not suit—or so they claim—but even they dare not ignore it. Nobody turns his back on the sea, not if he or she has any sense. And anyway, our true inclinations are just the opposite. We are—always have been—drawn to the sea. We can't help but recognize our love of it, or at least our awful fascination with it. And though we admit this to be so, *why* it is so is not so clear.

There are many and various suggestions on offer. Some people claim that since all life came from the sea, it is in fact our natural element, and that this accounts for our attraction to it. Others remind us of our early great-days afloat in the fluid of our mother's womb. The anthropologist and archeologist both will tell you that water-craft developed as the most efficient technology for reaping the sea's harvest, for projecting expeditions of exploration and immigration, for the carrying of trade, and for the prosecuting of war. At the same time, Bible scholars assert that we'd do well to meditate on Jonah's attempted flight from God by sailing ship, and praise the Lord that Jesus walked on water.

Introduction

In the end, any or all of this may be relevant so long as we also remember the awe-inspiring majesty and mystery of the sea itself, its dead calms and vaulting storms, the infinite variety of its sea-life, its salt sting and bracing airs, its immense and somehow life-affirming emptiness, and its terrible unforgivingness. All of this too is fundamental to the literature and the wisdom of the sea.

No little wonder then—to paraphrase Masefield—we feel as though we *gotta* go down to the sea in ships. But what are you to do if you have no sailboat handy? Suppose there is a *great* deal to occupy you on the land and you cannot simply sail away. What then? For that, dear Reader, I offer you this volume of *The Little Blue Book of Sailing Wisdom* to chew on. It's all here, the history, romance, adventure, mystery, lore, travel-log and ship-craft, bite-sized and ready to melt—or explode—in your mouth.

So read on. The wind blows fair. The taste is salt.

Stephen Vincent Brennan
New York, 2014

PART ONE

The Deep Blue Sea

We are as near to heaven by sea as by land.
—SIR HUMPHREY GILBERT

• • •

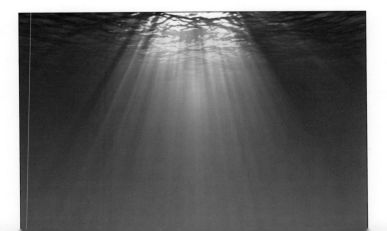

The sea all water, yet receives rain still,
And in abundance addeth to his store.
—WILLIAM SHAKESPEARE

• • •

A sure cure for seasickness is to sit under a tree.
—SPIKE MILLIGAN (TERENCE ALAN MILLIGAN)

• • •

And I looked upon the true sea—the sea that plays with men till their hearts are broken, and wears stout ships to death. Nothing can touch the brooding bitterness of its heart. Open to all and faithful to none, it exercises its fascination for the undoing of the best. To love it is not well. It knows no bond of plighted troth, no fidelity to misfortune, to long companionship, to long devotion. The promise it holds out perpetually is very great; but the only secret of its possession is strength, strength—the jealous, sleepless strength of a man guarding a coveted treasure within his gates.
—JOSEPH CONRAD
The Mirror of the Sea

• • •

Yea, foolish mortals, noah's flood is not yet subsided; two thirds of the fair world it yet covers.
—HERMAN MELVILLE
Moby Dick

• • •

For whatever we lose (like a you or a me), it's always ourselves we find in the sea.
—E. E. CUMMINGS

• • •

The water is the same on both sides of the ship.
—FINNISH SAILING PROVERB

• • •

It is a beauteous evening, calm and free;
The holy time is quiet as a nun
Breathless with adoration; the broad sun
Is sinking down in its tranquility;
The gentleness of heaven is on the Sea.
—WILLIAM WORDSWORTH
Poems in Two Volumes

• • •

It was the law of the sea, they said. Civilization ends at the water-line. Beyond that, we all enter the food chain, and not always at the top.
—HUNTER S. THOMPSON
Generation of Swine: Tales of Shame and Degradation in the '80s

• • •

I love to sail forbidden seas and land on barbarous coasts.
———HERMAN MELVILLE
Moby Dick

• • •

The sea is my brother.
———JACK KEROUAC
The Sea Is My Brother

• • •

The sea is mother-death and she is a mighty female, the one who
wins, the one who sucks us all up.
———ANNE SEXTON

• • •

The sea is the same as it has always been since men ever went on it in boats.
——ERNEST HEMINGWAY

• • •

The sea finds out everything you did wrong.
——FRANCIS STOKES

• • •

The sea is common to us all.
——PLAUTUS

• • •

For all that has been said of the love that certain natures (on shore) have professed to feel for it, for all the celebrations it had been the object of in prose and song, the sea has never been friendly to man. At most it has been the accomplice of human restlessness.

—JOSEPH CONRAD
The Mirror of the Sea

• • •

I was set free! I dissolved in the sea, became white sails and flying spray, became beauty and rhythm, became moonlight and the ship and the high dim-starred sky! I belonged, without past or future, within peace and unity and a wild joy, within something greater than my own life, or the life of Man, to Life itself!

—EUGENE O'NEILL

Long Day's Journey into Night

● ● ●

Calm waters don't make a skillful sailor.

—ANONYMOUS

● ● ●

Men go back to the mountains, as they go back to sailing ships at sea, because in the mountains and on the sea they must face up.

—HENRY DAVID THOREAU

● ● ●

The sea, once it casts its spell, holds one in its net of wonder forever.

—JACQUES-YVES COUSTEAU

• • •

The sea—this truth must be confessed—has no generosity. No display of manly qualities—courage, hardihood, endurance, faithfulness—has ever been known to touch its irresponsible consciousness of power.

—JOSEPH CONRAD
The Mirror of the Sea

• • •

Blue, green grey, white, or black: smooth, ruffled, or mountainous; that ocean is not silent.

—H. P. LOVECRAFT

• • •

The Deep Blue Sea

So what remains? The ocean that lies dark
Around, and the blessed islands. Come, embark.
——HORACE
Epode 16. 41–2

• • •

The fair breeze blew, the white foam flew,
The furrows followed free;
We were the first that ever burst
Into that silent sea.
——SAMUEL TAYLOR COLERIDGE
"The Rime of the Ancient Mariner"

• • •

It is an interesting biological fact that all of us have in our veins
the exact percentage of salt in our blood that exists in the ocean,
and therefore, we have salt in our blood, in our sweat, in our
tears. We are tied to the ocean. And when we go back to the
sea—whether it is to sail or to watch it—we are going back from
whence we came.
——JOHN FITZGERALD KENNEDY

• • •

The sea never changes and its works, for all the talk of men, are wrapped in mystery.
——JOSEPH CONRAD
Typhoon

• • •

I'll drown more sailors than the mermaid shall.
——WILLIAM SHAKESPEARE
Henry VI

• • •

Roll on, thou deep and dark blue ocean—roll!
——LORD BYRON

• • •

The sea is as near as we come to another world.
——ANNE STEVENSON

• • •

Not to have control over the senses is like sailing in a rudderless ship, bound to break to pieces on coming in contact with the very first rock.
——MAHATMA GANDHI

• • •

This song the sea sings strikes the inner ear
O'erlaid and deafened by the city's din,
The odours of the sea and down let in
Lost thoughts of many an ancient hope and fear:
The wind blows through me, carrying clean away
The dust that long has settled on my heart—
——WALTER HOGG
"Sea Change"

• • •

Ocean: A body of water occupying about two-thirds of a world made for man—who has no gills.
——AMBROSE BIERCE

• • •

The snot green sea. The scrotum tightening sea.
—JAMES JOYCE
Ulysses

• • •

Why do we love the sea? It is because it has some potent power to make us think things we like to think.
—ROBERT HENRI

• • •

The sea hates a coward.
—EUGENE O'NEILL
Mourning Becomes Electra

• • •

We sailed forth and soon came upon another island, but because of shallows and broken stone and the fury of the seas, we bore off and beached our skin ship instead upon a rock, where nothing grew, a small desolate island. Or so we thought, for when we lit the fire so that we might bake our grain and dress our meat, the island began to move under us. And all a panic then, amazed and full of fear, we threw ourselves into the boat, and pulled and twisted at the oars, swatting and thumping one another in our haste to be away. And lo, the island seemed to dip and we floated free and soon were well away. And all that night we spied the beacon of our fire leaping and dancing in the cold, dark ocean. Brendan must have smelled the terror on us, for he said, *"Do not be afraid. It is only a great fish, the biggest in the sea. He labors night and day to swallow his own tail, but he cannot because of his great size. He is called Jasconius."*

——TRANSLATED BY STEPHEN VINCENT BRENNAN
The Voyages of Saint Brendan

• • •

Water, water, everywhere,
And all the boards did shrink;
Water, water, everywhere,
Nor any drop to drink.
——SAMUEL TAYLOR COLERIDGE
"The Rime of the Ancient Mariner"

• • •

Who is staring at the sea is already sailing a little.
——PAUL CARVEL

• • •

The sea hath no king but God alone.
——DANTE GABRIEL ROSSETTI
"The White Ship"

• • •

The Gulf Stream water is of the darkest sapphire blue, which seems to have no trace of green in it, such as there is in other parts of the Atlantic. As one approaches the northern limit of the Stream, curious patches of brownish-green water appear in the blue and, when one has actually left the Stream and is sailing in the waters which flow south from the Arctic, this brownish-green color is very noticeable.

—E. G. MARTIN
Deep Water Cruising

• • •

A man who is not afraid of the sea will soon be drowned.

———JOHN MILLINGTON SYNGE

The Aran Islands

● ● ●

The boisterous sea of liberty in never without a wave.

———THOMAS JEFFERSON

● ● ●

There is nothing so desperately monotonous as the sea, and I no
longer wonder at the cruelty of pirates.
—JAMES RUSSELL LOWELL

• • •

O'er the glad waters of the dark blue sea,
Our thoughts as boundless, and our souls are free
Far as the breeze can bear, the billows foam,
Survey our empire, and behold our home!
These are our realms, no limits to their sway—
Our flag the scepter all who meet obey.
—LORD BYRON
The Corsair

• • •

There is nothing more enticing, disenchanting, and enslaving than the life at sea.
—JOSEPH CONRAD
Lord Jim

● ● ●

Follow the river and you will find the sea.
—FRENCH PROVERB

● ● ●

There's fish in the sea, no doubt of it,
As good as ever came out of it.
—ANONYMOUS

• • •

There is nothing quite so good as burial at sea. It is simple, tidy,
and not very incriminating.
—ALFRED HITCHCOCK

• • •

A dark,
Illimitable ocean without bound,
Without dimension, where length, breadth, and height
And time and place are lost.
—JOHN MILTON
"Paradise Lost"

• • •

The Deep Blue Sea

In certain places, at certain hours, gazing at the sea is dangerous.
It is what looking at a woman sometimes is.
—VICTOR HUGO

• • •

He that will learn to pray, let him go to sea.
—GEORGE HERBERT

• • •

"Wouldst thou"—so the helmsman answered,
"Learn the secret of the sea?
Only those who brave its dangers
Comprehend its mystery!"
—HENRY WADSWORTH LONGFELLOW

• • •

There isn't any symbolism. The sea is the sea. The old man is an old man. The boy is a boy and the fish is a fish. The sharks are all sharks no better and no worse. All the symbolism people say is shit. What goes beyond is what you see beyond when you know.
—ERNEST HEMINGWAY, ON *THE OLD MAN AND THE SEA*

• • •

The Deep Blue Sea

Thou art the same, eternal sea!
The earth hath many shapes and forms
Of hill and valley, flower and tree;
Fields that the fervid noontide warms,
Or Winter's rugged grasp deforms,
Or bright with Autumn's golden store;
Thou coverest up thy face with storms,
Or smilest serene—but still thy roar
And dashing foam go up to vex the sea-beat shore.
—GEORGE LUNT

• • •

And then again we pulled our hide boat upon God's ocean,
and for three full days the wind blew foul, and then a sudden
all grew still. The wind blew not and the sea calmed and
flattened and seemed to set into a thing solid. And Brendan
said *"Brothers, lay off your oars, let us drift; and in this show true
submission to the will of God."*
—STEPHEN VINCENT BRENNAN
A Chronicle of the Voyages of Saint Brendan

• • •

Why did they make birds so delicate and fine as those sea swallows when the ocean can be so cruel? She is kind and very beautiful. But she can be so cruel and it comes so suddenly and such birds that fly, dipping and hunting, with their small sad voices are made too delicately for the sea.

——ERNEST HEMINGWAY
The Old Man and the Sea

• • •

The morning air blows fresh on him:
The waves dance gladly in his sight;
The sea-birds call, and wheel, and skim—
O, blessed morning light!
He doth not hear their joyous call; he sees
No beauty in the wave, nor feels the breeze.

——RICHARD HENRY DANA

• • •

PART TWO

Seamen and Women

Sigh no more, ladies, sigh no more,
Men are deceivers ever,
One foot in sea and one on shore,
To one thing constant never.
—WILLIAM SHAKESPEARE
Much Ado About Nothing

• • •

I was born in the breezes, and I had studied the sea as perhaps
few men have studied it, neglecting all else.
—CAPTAIN JOSHUA SLOCUM

• • •

Let me shipwreck in your thighs.
—DYLAN THOMAS
Under Milk Wood

• • •

I fear thee, ancient Mariner!
I fear thy skinny hand!
And thou art long, and lank, and brown,
As the ribbed sea-sand.
—SAMUEL TAYLOR COLERIDGE
"The Rime of the Ancient Mariner"

• • •

Wind is to us what money is to life on shore.
——STERLING HAYDEN

• • •

Separately there was only wind, water, sail, and hull, but at my hand the four had been given purpose and direction.
——LOWELL THOMAS

• • •

Wild nights!—Wild nights!
Were I with thee
Wild nights should be
Our luxury!

Futile—the winds—
To a heart in port—
Done with a compass—
Done with the chart—

Rowing in Eden—
Ah, the sea!
Might I but moor—tonight—
In thee!
—EMILY DICKINSON
"Wild Nights"

• • •

A man should learn to sail in all winds.
—ITALIAN PROVERB

● ● ●

Only the guy who isn't rowing has time to rock the boat.
—JEAN-PAUL SARTRE

● ● ●

Seamen and Women

Voyaging belongs to seaman, and to the wanderers of the world
who cannot, or will not, fit in.

——STERLING HAYDEN

• • •

I fully must know now
What race ye belong to. Ye far-away dwellers,
Sea-faring sailors, my simple opinion
Hear ye and hearken: haste is most fitting
Plainly to tell me what place ye are come from.

——BEOWULF

• • •

A great pilot can sail even when his canvas is torn.
—SENECA

• • •

In meantime flew our ships, and straight we fetch'd
The Siren's isle; a spleenless wind so stretch'd
Her wings to waft us, and so urged our keel.
But having reach'd this isle we could not feel
The least gasp of it, it was stricken dead,
And all the sea in prostrate slumber spread,
The Siren's devil charmed all. Up then flew
My friends to work, struck sail, together drew,
And under hatches stow'd them, sat, and plied
The polished oars, and did in curls divide
The white-head waters.
—HOMER, TRANSLATED BY GEORGE CHAPMAN
The Odyssey

• • •

Seamen and Women

The yarns of seamen have a direct simplicity, the whole meaning
of which lies within the shell of a cracked nut.

—JOSEPH CONRAD
Heart of Darkness

• • •

How little do the landsmen know
What we poor sailors feel,
When waves do mount, and winds do blow!
But we have hearts of steel.
No danger can afright us,
No enemy can flout;
We'll make the Monsieurs right us;
So put the can about.

—ANONYMOUS

• • •

Traditions of the Royal Navy? I'll give you traditions of the
Navy—rum, buggery, and the lash.
—ALLEGEDLY, WINSTON CHURCHILL TO THE BOARD OF THE
ADMIRALTY IN 1939

• • •

I shall no more to sea, to sea,
Here shall I die ashore—
This is a very scurvy tune to sing at a man's funeral: well, here's
my comfort. *[drinks.]*

The master, the swabber, the boatswain, and I,
The gunner, and his mate,
Lov'd Mall, Meg, and Marian, and Margery
But none of us car'd for Kate:
For she had a tongue with a tang,
Would cry to a sailor, Go, hang:
She lov'd not the savour of tar nor of pitch,
Yet a tailor might scratch her where-e'er she did itch:
Then to sea, boys, and let her go hang.

This is a scurvy tune too: But here's my comfort. *[drinks.]*
—STEPHANO, WILLIAM SHAKESPEARE
The Tempest

• • •

To be truly challenging, a voyage, like a life, must rest on a firm foundation of financial unrest. Otherwise you are doomed to a routine traverse, the kind known to yachtsmen, who play with their boats at sea—"cruising," it is called. Voyaging belongs to seamen, and to the wanderers of the world who cannot, or will not, fit in.

—STERLING HAYDEN
Wanderer

• • •

He was one of those men who are picked up at need in the ports of the world. They are competent enough, appear hopelessly hard up, show no evidence of any sort of vice, and carry about them all the signs of manifest failure. They come aboard on an emergency, care for no ship afloat, live in their own atmosphere of casual connection amongst their shipmates who know nothing of them, and make up their minds to leave at inconvenient times. They clear out with no words of leavetaking in some God-forsaken port other men would fear to be stranded in, and go ashore in company of a shabby sea-chest, corded like a treasure-box, and with an air of shaking the ship's dust off their feet.

—JOSEPH CONRAD
Typhoon

• • •

Seamen and Women

Sing fare you well my bonny young girl.
Hurrah, sing fare you well.
Oh fare you well, I wish you well.
Hurrah, sing fare you well.

Oh fare you well, we're bound away.
Hurrah, sing fare you well.
We're bound away across the bay
Hurrah, sing fare you well.

We're bound away to Mobile Bay
Hurrah, sing fare you well.
With you I can no longer stay.
Hurrah, sing fare you well.

Oh fare you well, we're bound away
Hurrah, sing fare you well.
With you I can no longer stay.
Hurrah, sing fare you well.

I'm coming back to you one day,
Hurrah, sing fare you well.
I'm coming back with three months' pay.
Hurrah, sing fare you well.

——NINETEENTH CENTURY SEA CHANTEY "FARE YOU WELL"

• • •

There be three things which are too wonderful for me, yea, four
things which I know not:
The way of an eagle in the air; the way of a serpent upon a rock;
the way of a ship in the midst of the sea; and the way of a man
with a maid.
—PROVERBS 30: 18-19 AV

• • •

The cure for everything is salt water—sweat, tears, or the sea.
—ISAK DINESEN

• • •

42

Orpheus replied: "I have been instructed in a dream to sail with
you. Let us go aboard."
—ROBERT GRAVES
Hercules, My Shipmate

• • •

When Nelson attempted to get compensation for the loss of his
eye, he was told that no money could be paid without a surgeon's
certificate. Annoyed by this petty bureaucracy—his wounds were
well known—he nevertheless obtained the documentation. At
the same time he requested the surgeon to make out a second
certificate attesting to the obvious loss of his arm. He presented
the document and was paid out the appropriate sum. Com-
menting on the paucity of the sum, he said "Oh this is only for an
eye. In a few days I shall come back for an arm, and probably, in
a little while longer, for a leg." Later that week he returned to the
clerk's office and solemnly handed over a second certificate.
—APOCRYPHAL TALE OF THE GREAT SEA-LORD

• • •

Candidus in nauta turpis color: aequoris unda
Debet et a radiis sideris esse niger.
*(For a white skin on a sailor is a disgrace: owing to the saltwater
and the rays of the sun he should be dark-skinned.)*
—OVID
Ars Amatoria

• • •

I have great comfort from this fellow: methinks he hath no
drowning mark upon him; his complexion is perfect gallows.
—WILLIAM SHAKESPEARE
The Tempest

• • •

Seamen and Women

A sailor is born, not made. And by "sailor" is meant, not the average efficient and hopeless creature who is found to-day in the forecastle of deepwater ships, but the man who will take a fabric compounded of wood and iron and rope and canvas and compel it to obey his will on the surface of the sea. Barring captains and mates of big ships, the small-boat sailor is the real sailor. He knows—he must know—how to make the wind carry his craft from one given point to another given point. He must know about tides and rips and eddies, bar and channel markings, and day and night signals; he must be wise in weather-lore; and he must be sympathetically familiar with the peculiar qualities of his boat which differentiate it from every other boat that was ever built and rigged. He must know how to gentle her about, as one instance of a myriad, and to fill her on the other tack without deadening her way or allowing her to fall off too far.

—JACK LONDON
The Human Drift

• • •

To lay aloft in a howling breeze
May tickle a landsman's taste,
But the happiest hour a sailor sees
Is when he's down at an inland town,
With his Nancy on his knees, yeo-ho!
And his arm around her waist!

—W. S. GILBERT
The Mikado

• • •

At the piping of all hands,
When the judgment signal's spread—
When the islands and the lands,
And the seas give up the dead,
And the south and the north shall come;
When the sinner is dismay'd,
And the just man is afraid,
Then heaven be thy aid,
Poor Tom.
——BRAINARD

• • •

It would be difficult to describe the subtle brotherhood of men that was here established on the seas. No one said that it was so. No one mentioned it. But it dwelt in the boat, and each man felt it warm him.
——STEPHEN CRANE
The Open Boat

• • •

They'll tell thee, sailors, when away,
In ev'ry port a mistress find.
——JOHN GAY
Sweet William's Farewell to Black-Eyed Susan

• • •

Seamen and Women

Lieutenant Bush: It is the captain's wish, Your Ladyship, that from now on you and your maid remain below.
Lady Wellesley: *[to Hornblower]* Can two women really be so distracting, captain?
Captain Hornblower: May I remind you that my men have been continously at sea for eight months?
Lady Wellesley: *[as Hornblower begins to walk away]* Oh, captain! *[He stops and turns to her]*
Lady Wellesley: And how long have you been at sea?
Captain Hornblower: Ha-H'mmm!

—C. S. FORESTER
Captain Hornblower (film)

• • •

"I'll have you know I do the swearing on this ship.
If I need your assistance I'll call you."
—JACK LONDON / CAPT. WOLF LARSEN
The Sea Wolf

• • •

But the standing toast that pleased the most
Was—The wind that blows, the ship that goes,
And the lass that loves a sailor.
—CHARLES DIBDIN
The Lass That Loves a Sailor

• • •

THE LITTLE BLUE BOOK OF SAILING WISDOM

My bounty is as boundless as the sea,
My love as deep; the more I give to thee,
The more I have, for both are infinite.
—WILLIAM SHAKESPEARE
Romeo and Juliet

• • •

Once more upon the waters! Yet once more!
And the waves beneath me as a steed
That knows his rider.
——LORD BYRON

• • •

A man is never lost at sea.
——ERNEST HEMINGWAY
The Old Man and the Sea

• • •

I once knew a writer who, after saying beautiful things about
the sea, passed through a Pacific Hurricane, and he became a
changed man.
——CAPTAIN JOSHUA SLOCUM

• • •

PART THREE

Ship

I want a boat that drinks 6, eats 4, and sleeps 2.

——ERNEST K. GANN

• • •

Hoist up the sail while the gale doth last,
Tide and wind stay no man's pleasure.

——ROBERT SOUTHWELL

• • •

Ship

The sail, the play of its pulse so like our own lives: so thin and yet so full of life, so noiseless when it labors hardest, so noisy and impatient when least effective.

—HENRY DAVID THOREAU
A Week on the Concord and Merrimack Rivers

• • •

One ship is very much like another, and the sea is always the same. In the immutability of their surroundings the foreign shores, the foreign faces, the changing immensity of life, glide past, veiled not by a sense of mystery but by a slightly disdainful ignorance; for there is nothing mysterious to a seaman unless it be the sea itself, which is the mistress of his existence and as inscrutable as Destiny.

—JOSEPH CONRAD
Heart of Darkness

• • •

Behold the threaden sails,
Borne with the invisible and creeping wind,
Draw the bottoms through the furrow'd sea,
Breasting the lofty surge.

—WILLIAM SHAKESPEARE
King Henry V

• • •

The best cruising yacht is a conglomeration of compromise.
——JOHN IRVING

• • •

It is often said that a man's boat is an extension of himself, but that is not quite true. A man's boat is more an instrument by which his self is exposed.
——ADAM NICOLSON
Seamanship

• • •

Give me a spirit that on this life's rough seas
Loves to have his sails filled with a lusty wind,
Even till his sail-yards tremble, his masts crack
And his rapt ship run on her side so low
That she drinks water, and her keel plows air.
——GEORGE CHAPMAN

• • •

Throw no shot away. Aim every one. Keep cool. Work steadily. Fire into her quarters—main deck to main deck, quarterdeck to quarterdeck. Don't try to dismast her. Kill the men and the ship is yours.

—CAPTAIN PHILIP BROKE, BEFORE ACTION AGAINST THE *USS CHESAPEAKE*

• • •

There are only two colors to paint a boat, black or white, and only a fool would paint a boat black.

—NATHANAEL G. HERRESHOFF

• • •

I wish to have no connection with any ship that does not sail fast;
for I intend to go in harm's way.
—JOHN PAUL JONES, IN A 1778 LETTER TO LE RAY DE CHAUMONT

● ● ●

There is but a plank between a sailor and eternity.
—THOMAS GIBBONS

● ● ●

Ship

I march across great waters like a queen,
I whom so many wisdoms helped to make;
Over the uncruddled billows of sea green
I blanch the bubbled highway of my wake.
By me my wandering tenants clasp the hands
And know the thoughts of men in other lands.
                    —JOHN MASEFIELD
          Salt-Water Poems and Ballads

• • •

The *Gull* was a plank-on-edge cutter of ancient vintage. She had a tremendous jackyard topsail, a terrific tiller, and a pack of wild Irishmen aboard her, who flogged the life out of her.

—ALFRED F. LOOMIS
Ocean Racing

• • •

The twist-stemmed vessel had traveled such distance
That the sailing-men saw the sloping embankments,
The sea cliffs gleaming, precipitous mountains,
Nesses enormous: they were nearing the limits
At the end of the ocean.

—BEOWULF

• • •

Ship

The ring-stemmèd vessel,
Bark of the atheling, lay there at anchor,
Icy in glimmer and eager for sailing.
—BEOWULF

• • •

The nature of a voyage is set before you cast off. A sea passage is shaped by the boat's time attached to the land.
—ADAM NICOLSON
Seamanship

• • •

When the adverse fleets approach each other, the *courses* are commonly hauled up in the *brails*, and the *topgallant sails* and *stay sail* furled. The movement of each ship is chiefly regulated by the *main* and *fore topsails*, and the *jib*; the *mizzen topsail* being reserved to hasten or retard the course of the ship, and, in fine, by backing or filling, hoisting or lowering it, to determine her velocity.
—W. BURNEY
New Universal Dictionary of the Marine, 1815

• • •

Traditionally, the twenty-four hour day at sea is split up into
seven parts, known as watches and are named as follows:

Midnight to 4 a.m.	Middle Watch
4 a.m. to 8 a.m.	Morning Watch
8 a.m. to Noon	Forenoon Watch
Noon to 4 p.m.	Afternoon Watch
4 p.m. to 6 p.m.	First Dog Watch
6 p.m. to 8 p.m.	Last or Second Dog Watch
8 p.m. to Midnight	First Watch

With two exceptions each of these Watches are four hours in
length; but the two Dog Watches are only two hours each.

—DOUGLAS SERVICE

• • •

For two centuries, 1622 to 1825, the official diet of the Royal
Navy consisted of beer, salt pork and salt beef, oatmeal, dried
peas, butter and cheese, usually rancid, and biscuit that walked by
itself, as Roderick Random tells in Smollett's novel, by virtue of
the worms that made it their home.

—BARBARA W. TUCHMAN
First Salute: A View of the American Revolution

• • •

Ship

Sailing in heavy weather may be a test of seaman's nerve, but drifting in the lightest of airs is a test of his skill and of his temper.

—JOHN IRVING

● ● ●

A small sailing craft is not only beautiful, it is seductive and full of strange promise and the hint of trouble.

—E. B. WHITE
The Sea and the Wind That Blows

● ● ●

And then went down to the ship,
Set keel to breakers, forth on the godly sea, and
We set up the mast and sail on that swart ship,
Bore sheep aboard her, and our bodies also
Heavy with weeping, and the winds from sternward
Bore us out onward with bellying canvas.

—EZRA POUND
Canto I

● ● ●

If you already have a ship and she seems to be almost what you want—keep her. There may be a better ship out there, but there is certainly a worse one.

—TRADITIONAL SAILOR'S SAYING

• • •

Set he out on his vessel,
To drive on the deep, Dane-country left he.
Along by the mast then a sea-garment fluttered,
A rope-fastened sail. The sea-boat resounded,
The wind o'er the waters the wave-floater nowise
Kept from its journey; the sea-goer traveled,
The foamy-necked floated forth o'er the currents,
The well-fashioned vessel o'er the ways of the ocean,

—BEOWULF

• • •

Ship

Sail forth—steer for the deep waters only.
Reckless, O soul, exploring,I with thee and thou with me.
And we will risk the ship, ourselves, and all.
—WALT WHITMAN
"Passage to India"

• • •

This is the Blue Postesses
Where the Midshipmen leave their chestesses,
They call for tea and toastesses,
And, alack, forget to pay for their breakfastesses.
—RECALLED AS GRAFFITI SCRATCHED ON A WINDOW OF THE BLUE
POSTS INN, IN PORTSMOUTH, NINETEENTH CENTURY

• • •

I lay in the bowsprit, with the water foaming into spume under
me, the masts with every sail white in the moonlight towering
above me. I became drunk with the beauty and singing rhythm
of it, and for a moment lost myself—actually lost my life.
—EUGENE O'NEILL
Long Day's Journey into Night

• • •

I start from the premise that no object created by man is as
satisfying to his body and soul as a proper sailing yacht.
—ARTHUR BEISER
The Proper Yacht

• • •

Shipboard comfort is achieved by reducing luxuries, not by
increasing them.
—ANONYMOUS

• • •

Land was created to provide a place for boats to visit.
—BROOKS ATKINSON

• • •

A goodly paint job may cover a multitude of sins, but murder
will out.
—ANONYMOUS

• • •

O youth! The strength of it, the faith of it, the imagination of
it! To me she was not an old rattle-trap carting about the world
a lot of coal for a freight—to me she was the endeavor, the test,
the trial of life. I think of her with pleasure, with affection, with
regret—as you would think of someone dead who you have
loved. I shall never forget her . . . Pass the bottle.
—JOSEPH CONRAD
Youth, A Narrative

• • •

Ships are the nearest things to dreams that hands have ever made.
—ROBERT N. ROSE

• • •

Navigation (that useful part of Mathamaticks) is a Science which has been highly valued by the Antients, especially by our Ancestors of this Island; it being the beauty and bulwork of England, the Wall and Wealth of Britain, and the bridge that joins it to the Universe.
—JOHN SELLER
Practical Navigation

• • •

Ship

I have had to pass a considerable portion of my life aboard small craft of various kinds, and after a long and mixed experience of the life, I have come to two very definite conclusions concerning it. One is that life on a small boat in fine weather is the only kind of life worth living. The other is that, in bad weather, it's just plain hell.

—WESTON MARTYR
The Southseaman: The Life Story of a Schooner

• • •

Let your boat of life be light, packed with only what you need: a homely home and simple pleasures, one or two friends, worth the name, someone to love and someone to love you, a cat, a dog, and a pipe or two, enough to eat and enough to wear, and a little more than enough to drink; for thirst is a dangerous thing.

—JEROME K. JEROME
Three Men in a Boat

• • •

For the man with his height of eye at 8 feet above sea-level, the sea horizon will be distant about 3 ¼ miles.

—COMMANDER JOHN IRVING, RN

• • •

For the first time, and not on paper and in dreams, I had the little ship alone in my hands in a night of velvet dark below and stars above, pushing steadily along into unknown waters. I was extremely happy.

—ARTHUR RANSOME

• • •

If you wish to build a ship, don't gather people to collect wood, and don't assign tasks and jobs, but rather teach them to long for the endless immensity of the sea.

—ANTOINE DE SAINT-EXUPÉRY

• • •

After long periods without sleep, a healthy young man likes to make it up by sleeping for fourteen hours or so at a stretch. But the routine of watch-keeping makes this impossible on a ship.

—RICHARD HUGHES
In Hazard

• • •

Ship

Gear which falls from aloft is usually harder than the head
it fell upon.
——PROVERB

• • •

Boats, like whiskey, are all good.
——R. D. CULLER

• • •

If you can not arrive in daylight, then stand off well clear, and
wait until dawn. After all, that's one of the things God made
boats for—to wait in.
——TRISTAN JONES

• • •

The essentials of a good ship are a tight hull, good gear, and a
reliable engine.
——JOHN IRVING

• • •

A Yankee ship came down the river
Blow, boys, blow
Her masts did bend, her sails did shiver
Blow, bully boys, blow
Her sails were old, her sides were rotten
Blow, boys, blow
Her charts her skipper had forgotten
Blow, bully boys, blow
——SEA CHANTEY
"Blow, Bully Boys, Blow"

● ● ●

The desire to build a house is the tired wish of a man content
thenceforward with a single anchorage. The desire to build a boat
is the desire of youth, unwilling yet to accept the idea of a final
resting place.
——ARTHUR RANSOME

● ● ●

Design has taken the place of what sailing used to be.
——DENNIS CONNOR

• • •

When a man weighs anchor in a little ship or a large one he does a jolly thing! He cuts himself off and he starts for freedom and for the chance of things.
——HILAIRE BELLOC
The Cruise of the "Nona"

• • •

It is a wise ship that keeps out of the way of anything a great deal bigger than herself.
——COMMANDER JOHN IRVING, RN

• • •

Being in a ship is being in a jail, with the chance of being drowned.
——DR. SAMUEL JOHNSON

• • •

Never a ship sails out of a bay, but carries my heart as a stowaway.
——ROSELLE MERCIER MONTGOMERY

• • •

The ship was cheered, the harbor cleared,
Merrily did we drop
Below the kirk, below the hill,
Below the lighthouse top.
——SAMUEL TAYLOR COLERIDGE
"The Rime of the Ancient Mariner"

• • •

Ship

Overhead, the white sails stretched their arms to catch the night wind. They were my sails—my wings—and they had brought me to the sea of my boyhood dreams.

—WILLIAM ROBINSON
Building a Little Ship

• • •

It is not the ship so much as the skillful sailing that assures the prosperous voyage.

—GEORGE WILLIAM CURTIS

• • •

Timid men prefer the calm of despotism to the tempestuous sea of liberty.

—THOMAS JEFFERSON

• • •

Dear God! My boat is very small and thy sea so very wide.
Have Mercy!
—BRETON FISHERMAN'S PRAYER

• • •

The Liner she's a lady, an' she never
looks nor 'eeds,—
The Man-o-War's 'er 'usband, an' 'e
gives 'er all she needs,
But, oh, the little cargo boats that sail
the wet seas roun',
They're just the same as you an' me
a plyin' up and down!
—RUDYARD KIPLING
"The Liner, She's a Lady"

• • •

Ship

As idle as a painted ship
Upon a painted ocean.
——SAMUEL TAYLOR COLERIDGE
"The Rime of the Ancient Mariner"

• • •

The goal is not to sail the boat, but rather to help the boat
sail herself.
——JOHN ROUSMANIERE

• • •

A wet sheet and a flowing sea,
A wind that follows fast
And fills the white and rustling sail
And bends the gallant mast.
——ALLAN CUNNINGHAM

• • •

Ship

Here's my journey's end, here is my butt,
And very sea-mark of my utmost sail.
———WILLIAM SHAKESPEARE
Othello

• • •

There is *nothing*—absolutely nothing—half so much worth
doing as simply messing about in boats.
———KENNETH GRAHAME
The Wind in the Willows

• • •

Ships are but boards, sailors but men: there be land-rats, and water-rats, water-thieves, and land-thieves; I mean pirates; and then, there is the peril of waters, winds and rocks: the man is, notwithstanding, sufficient;—three thousand ducats;—I think I may take his bond.

—WILLIAM SHAKESPEARE
The Merchant of Venice

• • •

I kept my eyes on every ship we passed. Until the previous day, I had never seen a square-rigged vessel; and no enthusiast in the arts ever gloated on a fine picture or statue with greater avidity than my soul drank in the wonder and beauty of every ship I passed.

—JAMES FENIMORE COOPER
Afloat and Ashore

• • •

Ship

Setting the sails by no means ends the work at them. Trimming is quite as important. Every time there is the slightest shift in the course or wind there ought to be a corresponding shift of trim so as to catch every breath the sail can hold. To effect this with the triangular sails a sheet must be slacked away or hauled more in; while, in the case of the square sails on the yards, a brace must be attended to.

—WILLIAM WOOD
All Afloat

• • •

Sound trumpets, ho!—weigh anchor—loosen sail—
The seaward-flying banners chide delay;
As if't were heaven that breathes this kindly gale,
Our life-like bark beneath it speeds away.—

—PINKNEY

• • •

There was something inexpressibly sad in this. It seemed like standing at the death-bed of an old friend. The sea was still heaving violently; the gale, although moderated, was still pretty stiff, and the sun was setting in wild lurid clouds when the *Foam* rose for the last time—every spar and rope standing out sharply against the sky. Then she bent forward slowly, as she overtopped a huge billow. Into the hollow she rushed. Like an expert diver she went down head foremost into the deep, and, next moment, those who had so lately trod her deck saw nothing around them save the lowering sky and the angry waters of the Pacific Ocean.

—R. M. BALLANTYNE
Sunk at Sea

● ● ●

Steam has not banished from the deep sea the ships that lift tall spires of canvas to win their way from port to port. The gleam of their topsails recalls the centuries in which men wrought with stubborn courage to fashion fabrics of wood and cordage that should survive the enmity of the implacable ocean and make the winds obedient. Their genius was unsung, their hard toil forgotten, but with each generation the sailing ship became nobler and more enduring, until it was a perfect thing.

—RALPH D. PAINE
The Singular Fate of the Brig Polly

● ● ●

Ship

The heads of square sails are made fast to yards, which are at right angles to the masts on which they pivot. Sails and yards are raised, lowered, swung at the proper angle to catch the wind, and held in place by halliards, lifts, braces, and sheets, which can be worked from the deck. Sheets are ropes running from the lower corners of sails. All upper sails have their sheets running through sheave-holes in the yardarms next below, then through quarter-blocks underneath these yards and beside the masts, and then down to the deck. Braces are the ropes which swing the yards to the proper angle. Halliards are those which hoist or lower both the yards and sails. The square sails themselves are controlled by drawlines called clew-garnets running up from the lower corners, leechlines running in diagonally from the middle of the outside edges, buntlines running up from the foot, and spilling lines, to spill the wind in heavy weather. When the area of a sail has to be reduced, it is reefed by gathering up the head, if a square sail, or the foot, if triangular, and tying the gathered-up part securely by reef points, that is, by crossing and knotting the short lines on either side of this part. The square sails on the mainmast are called, when eight are carried, the mainsail, lower and upper maintopsails, lower and upper maintopgallants, main-royal, main-skysail, and the moonsail. The standing rigging is the whole assemblage of ropes by which the masts are supported.

—WILLIAM WOOD
All Afloat

• • •

PART FOUR

Storm and Calm

The hollow winds begin to blow.
——ANONYMOUS

• • •

A gigantic wave breaks violently over the jetty, raising a sparkling wash of spray, and . . . flows turbulently over the stones on the shore. Wave after wave breaks over the jetty, ever more violently, and . . . flows over the stones on the shore, ever more turbulently. The raging sea boils.

——SERGI EISENSTEIN
Battleship Potemkin

• • •

Storm and Calm

A clean wind, a tempering wind—that's all I ask!
—ANONYMOUS

• • •

In calms, Heaven laughs to see us languish thus.
—JOHN DONNE
"The Calm"

• • •

In the end, however perfect your boat, you go to sea exhausted,
when the weather is least suitable.
—ADAM NICOLSON
Seamanship

• • •

I'm not afraid of storms, for I'm learning to sail my ship.
—LOUISA MAY ALCOTT
Little Women

• • •

Sir W. Penn, who stayed to dine there, and did so; but the wind being high, the ship (though the motion of it was hardly discernable to the eye) did make me sick, so I could not eat anything almost . . . No sooner come into the yacht, though overjoyed at the good work we have done today, but I was overcome with seasickness so that I begun to spew soundly—and so continued a good while—till at last I went into the cabin, and shutting my eyes, my trouble did cease, that I fell asleep; which continued till we come into Chatham River, where the water was smooth, and then I rose and was very well.

—SAMUEL PEPYS
The Diary of Samuel Pepys: 1665

• • •

One wave already had come down on the deck, like a really vast oak crashing. A few more would sink the ship.

—RICHARD HUGHES
In Hazard

• • •

I would fain die a dry death.

—WILLIAM SHAKESPEARE
The Tempest

• • •

Storm and Calm

Off Cape Horn there are but two kinds of weather, neither one of them the pleasant kind.

—JOHN MASEFIELD

• • •

For my part I know of no difference between a Hurricane among the Carribee Islands in the *West Indies* and a Tuffoon upon the coast of *China* in the *East Indies*, but only the Name: And I am apt to believe that both Words have one signification, which is a *violent storm.*

—WILLIAM DAMPIER

• • •

Breath soft, ye winds! Ye waves in silence sleep.

—ANONYMOUS

• • •

Never hope to avoid a big following sea by running from it.
—TRADITIONAL SAILOR'S MAXIM

• • •

And he said unto them, I am an Hebrew; and I fear the LORD, the God of heaven, which hath made the sea and the dry land. Then were the men exceedingly afraid, and said unto him. Why hast thou done this? For the men knew that he fled from the presence of the LORD, because he had told them. Then said they unto him, What shall we do unto thee, that the sea may be calm unto us? for the sea wrought, and was tempestuous. And he said unto them, Take me up, and cast me forth into the sea; so shall the sea be calm unto you: for I know that for my sake this great tempest is upon you. Nevertheless the men rowed hard to bring it to the land; but they could not: for the sea wrought, and was tempestuous against them. Wherefore they cried unto the LORD, and said, We beseech thee, O LORD, we beseech thee, let us not perish for this man's life, and lay not upon us innocent blood: for thou, O LORD, hast done as it pleased thee. So they look up Jonah, and cast him forth into the sea: and the sea ceased from her raging.
—JONAH 1:1-15 AV

• • •

Storm and Calm

Never allow yourself to be left by weather or anything else in
a position from which it is risky to move and in which it is risky
to stay.

—JOHN IRVING

• • •

Any fool can carry on, but a wise man knows how to shorten sail
in time.

—JOSEPH CONRAD

• • •

Oh, many a dream was in the ship
An hour before her death;
And sight of home, with sighs disturbed
The sleeper's long drawn breath.

—JOHN WILSON
The Isle of Palms

• • •

Sailing in rough weather is what the sport is about.
—TED TURNER

• • •

Only two sailors, in my experience, never ran aground. One never left port, and the other was an atrocious liar.
—DON BAMFORD

• • •

Alas, the storm is come again! My best way is to creep under his gaberdine; there is no other shelter hereabouts: misery acquaints a man with strange bed-fellows.

—WILLIAM SHAKESPEARE
The Tempest

• • •

Few sailors can behold the ship in which they have sailed sinking before their eyes without the same emotion of distress and pity, almost, which the spectacle of a drowning man excites in them.

—WILLIAM CLARK RUSSELL
The Wreck of the Grosvenor

• • •

In rage deaf as the sea, hasty as fire.

—WILLIAM SHAKESPEARE
Richard II

• • •

For, while aloft the order those attend
To furl the mainsail, or on deck descend;
A sea, up-surging with stupendous roll,
To instant ruin seems to doom the whole:
O friends, secure your hold! Arion cries—
It comes all dreadful! down the vessel lies
Half buried sideways; while, beneath it tost,
Four seamen off the lee yard-arm are lost:
Torn with resistless fury from their hold,
In vain their struggling arms the yard enfold;
In vain to grapple flying ropes they try,
The ropes, alas! a solid gripe deny:
Prone on the midnight surge with panting breath
They cry for aid, and long contend with death;
High o'er their heads the rolling billows sweep,
And down they sink in everlasting sleep—
Bereft of pow'r to help, their comrades see
The wretched victims die beneath the lee,
With fruitless sorrow their lost state bemoan,
Perhaps, a fatal prelude to their own!
—WILLIAM FALCONER
"The Shipwreck"

• • •

Out of sight of land the sailor feels safe. It is the beach that
worries him.
—CHARLES G. DAVIS

The south and west winds joined, and, as they blew
Waves like a rolling trench before them threw.
Sooner than you read this line, did the gale,
Like shot, not feared till felt, our sails assail.
—JOHN DONNE
"The Storm"

I hate storms, but calms undermine my spirits.
—BERNARD MOITESSIER

• • •

Sea disasters have a way of happening in the most unsuitable
weather . . . It is quite understandable that no matter who you
are, when a ship is sinking, folk want off with a degree of speed
commonly referred to as in a hurry . . . In any case ladies carrying
pistols do not need your assistance as a firearm is a great aid in
securing a place in a lifeboat.
—J. P. DONLEAVY
The Unexpurgated Code

• • •

Being hove to in a long gale is the most boring way of being
terrified I know.

—DONALD HAMILTON

• • •

Usually when running, the following sea will give a ripe warning.
When it begins to rear ominously astern shorten down at once
and reduce speed. There is much less chance of misjudging the
time to shorten sail or heave-to when one is butting into dirty
weather than when one runs before it.

—JOHN IRVING
The Yachtsman's Weekend Book

• • •

Storm and Calm

Oh, they built the ship Titanic to sail the ocean blue,
And they thought they had a ship that the sea would ne'er come
through.
But by the Lord almighty's hand, that ship would never land.
It was sad when the great ship went down.

It was sad, it was sad, it was sad when the great ship went down
To the bottom of the—
Husbands and wives, little children lost their lives.
It was sad when the great ship went down.

Oh, they sailed away from England and were almost to the shore,
And the rich meanly refused to associate with the poor.
So they put them down below where they were the first to go.
It was sad when the great ship went down.

It was sad, it was sad, it was sad when the great ship went down
To the bottom of the—
Husbands and wives, little children lost their lives.
It was sad when the great ship went down.

Oh, they swung the lifeboats over the deep and raging sea.
And the band began a-playing "Nearer My God to Thee."
Little children wept and cried as the waves swept o'er the side
It was sad when the great ship went down.

—AMERICAN FOLK SONG

• • •

I saw only the gleaming crests of the waves. They showed white teeth while the sloop balanced over them. "Everything for an offing," I cried, and to this end I carried on all sail she would bear.

—CAPTAIN JOSHUA SLOCUM
Sailing Alone Around the World

• • •

Our storm is past, and that storm's tyrannous rage
A stupid calm, but nothing it doth 'suage.

—JOHN DONNE
"The Calm"

• • •

Storm and Calm

O Lord! methought what pain it was to drown!
What dreadful noise of water in mine ears!
What sights of ugly death within mine eyes!
Methought I saw a thousand fearful wracks:
A thousand men that fishes gnaw'd upon.

—WILLIAM SHAKESPEARE
King Richard III

• • •

These great seas bore down on the little cutter as though they were finally bent on her destruction. But she rose to them and fought her way through them in a way that made me want to sing a poem in her praise. Then, in a moment, I seemed engulfed in disaster . . . Suddenly I saw, towering above my limited horizon, ah huge wave, rearing its curling snowy crest so high that it dwarfed all others I had ever seen. I could hardly believe my eyes. It was a thing of beauty as well as of awe as it came roaring down upon us . . . Knowing that if I stayed on deck I would meet death by being washed overboard I just had time to climb into the rigging, and was about halfway up to the masthead when it burst upon the *Firecrest* in fury, burying her from my sight under tons of water and a lather of foam . . . Slowly she came out of the smother of it, and the great wave roared away to leeward. I slid down from my perch in the rigging . . .

—ALAIN GERBAULT
The Flight of the "Firecrest"

• • •

Prevention is, as in other aspects of seamanship, better than cure.
——SIR ROBIN KNOX-JOHNSTON

• • •

The Westerly Wind asserting his sway from the south-west
quarter is often like a monarch gone mad, driving forth with
wild imprecations the most faithful of his courtiers to shipwreck,
disaster, and death.
——JOSEPH CONRAD
The Mirror of the Sea

• • •

Anyone can hold the helm when the sea is calm.
——PROVERB

• • •

They fought with God's cold—
And they could not and fell to the deck
(Crushed them) or water (and drowned them) or rolled
With the sea-romp over the wreck.
——GERARD MANLEY HOPKINS
The Wreck of the Deutschland

• • •

If caught out badly in the open, remember that the sea will probably be worse nearer shore, and worse still in a harbor entrance.
——JOHN IRVING

• • •

I would give up part of my lifetime for the sake of knowing what is the average barometer reading in Paradise.
——LICHTENBERG

• • •

Storm and Calm

Nobody—not even Captain MacWhirr, who alone on deck had caught sight of a white line of foam coming on at such a height that he couldn't believe his eyes—nobody was to know the steepness of that sea and awful depth of the hollow the hurricane had scooped out behind the running wall of water.

—JOSEPH CONRAD
Typhoon

• • •

And now there came both mist and snow,
And it grew wondrous cold,
And ice, mast-high, came floating by,
As green as emerald.

—SAMUEL TAYLOR COLERIDGE
"The Rime of the Ancient Mariner"

• • •

The East Wind, an interloper in the dominions of Westerly weather, is an impassive-faced tyrant with a sharp poniard held behind his back for a treacherous stab.

—JOSEPH CONRAD
The Mirror of the Sea

• • •

But from the sea into the ship we turn,
Like parboil'd wretches, on the coals to burn.
Like Bajazet encaged, the shepherds scoff,
Or like slack-sinew'd Samson, his hair off,
Languish our ships.
—JOHN DONNE
"The Calm"

• • •

Two hours more we hang between life and "Davy Jones's Locker,"
when the storm breaks, though not so suddenly as when we
entered the vortex, and once again our ship is
staggering among the seas, jolting and butting against each other
like sheep driven along a strange road. The barometer is again
noted and found to be rising rapidly. Sail is made to steady ship
in the fearful sea, though there is but little wind to fill them. We
have got a breathing-spell and time to look about us.
—ARTHUR SINCLAIR
Two Years on the Alabama

• • •

Storm and Calm

Away in the loveable west,
On a pastoral forehead of Wales,
I was under a roof here, I was at rest,
And they the prey of the gales.
——GERARD MANLEY HOPKINS
The Wreck of the Deutschland

• • •

Facing it—always facing it—that's the way to get through.
—JOSEPH CONRAD
Typhoon

• • •

Seeing that a pilot guides the ship in which we sail, who will never allow us to perish even in the midst of shipwrecks, there is no reason why our minds should be overwhelmed with fear and overcome with weariness.
—JOHN CALVIN

• • •

Smoke rises vertically in a calm.

—ANONYMOUS

• • •

"Running all over the sea, trying to get behind the weather.
It's the maddest thing."

—JOSEPH CONRAD

Typhoon

• • •

The wind with us now, we sailed forth into the ocean; but soon fell a great tempest on us, which we were greatly troubled by for a long time and sorely belabored. And we saw, by the purveyance of God, a little island afar off, and full meekly we prayed to our Lord to send us thither in safety. It took eleven days, and in this time we monks were so weary of the long pull and the mountain gray oceans that we set little price upon our lives and cried continually to our Lord to show us mercy and bring us to that little island in safety.

—TRANSLATED BY STEPHEN VINCENT BRENNAN
The Voyages of Saint Brendan

• • •

Storm and Calm

Full fathom five thy father lies;
Of his bones are coral made;
These are pearls, that were his eyes:
Nothing of him that doth fade,
But doth suffer a sea-change
Into something rich and strange.
Sea-nymphs hourly ring his knell:
Hark! now I hear them,—ding-dong, bell.

—WILLIAM SHAKESPEARE
The Tempest

• • •

Waves are not measured in feet or inches, they are measured in increments of fear.
——BUZZY TRENT

• • •

While rocking winds are piping loud.
——JOHN MILTON
"Il Penseroso"

• • •

Storm and Calm

It's hard to eat, you're wet a lot of the time, and just going to the bathroom is a chore.

—TED TURNER, ON SAILING TO EUROPE IN A 38-FOOT BOAT

• • •

They hurried us aboard a bark;
Bore us some leagues to sea; where they prepared
A rotten carcass of a boat, not rigg'd,
Nor tackle, sail, nor mast: the very rats
Instinctively had girt us—
—WILLIAM SHAKESPEARE
Tempest

• • •

Captain Robbins could hardly speak when we gathered round
him on the forecastle, the seas breaking over the quarter-deck
in a way to render that sanctuary a very uncomfortable berth.
As soon as he could command himself, he told us that the ship
was hopelessly lost. How it had happened, he could not very well
explain himself, though he ascribed it to the fact that the currents
did not run in the direction in which, according to all sound
reasoning, they ought to run. This part of the speech was not
perfectly lucid, though, as I understood our unfortunate captain,
the laws of nature, owing to some inexplicable influence, had
departed, in some way or other, from their ordinary workings,
expressly to wreck the *John*. If this were not the meaning of what
he said, I did not understand this part of the address.

—JAMES FENIMORE COOPER
Afloat and Ashore

• • •

"Boatswain!"
"Here, master: what cheer?"
"Good: speak to the mariners; fall to 't
Yarely, or we run ourselves aground: bestir, bestir."

—WILLIAM SHAKESPEARE
Tempest

• • •

Storm and Calm

These waves were most wrongfully and barbarously
abrupt and tall, and each froth-top was a problem in
small-boat navigation.

—STEPHEN CRANE
The Open Boat

• • •

The yesty waves
Confound and swallow navigation up.

—WILLIAM SHAKESPEARE
Macbeth

• • •

For the first time, I now witnessed a tempest at sea. Gales, and pretty hard ones, I had often seen; but the force of the wind on this occasion, as much exceeded that in ordinary gales of wind, as the force of these had exceeded that of a whole-sail breeze. The seas seemed crushed, the pressure of the swooping atmosphere, as the currents of the air went howling over the surface of the ocean, fairly preventing them from rising; or, where a mound of water did appear, it was scooped up and borne off in spray, as the axe dubs inequalities from the log. In less than an hour after it began to blow the hardest, there was no very apparent swell—the deep breathing of the ocean is never entirely stilled—and the ship was as steady as if hove half out, her lower yard-arms nearly touching the water, an inclination at which they remained as steadily as if kept there by purchases. A few of us were compelled to go as high as the futtock-shrouds to secure the sails, but higher it was impossible to get. I observed that when I thrust out a hand to clutch anything, it was necessary to make the movement in such a direction as to allow for lee-way, precisely as a boat quarters the stream in crossing against a current. In ascending it was difficult to keep the feet on the ratlins, and in descending, it required a strong effort to force the body down towards the centre of gravity. I make no doubt, had I groped my way up to the cross-trees, and leaped overboard my body would have struck the water, thirty or forty yards from the ship. A marlin-spike falling from either top, would have endangered no one on deck.

—JAMES FENIMORE COOPER
Afloat and Ashore

• • •

PART FIVE

Weather-Eye

Given a good barometer and eyes, a sea forecaster has all the instruments he or she requires. Of all the weather systems there are variations and combinations, but whatever these may be, and however complicated, these portents remain always constant. The changing sky, the fluctuating glass, the signs and beacons which nature plants in the heavens—these are always there in a more or less marked degree. Out at sea there is never a lack of indication of what tricks nature has in her store.

—ANONYMOUS

• • •

If the wind be north-east, three days without rain.
Eight days will pass before south again.
—TRADITIONAL SEAMAN'S WEATHER AXIOM

• • •

No dew after sun,
Fine weather's on the run.
—TRADITIONAL SEAMAN'S WEATHER AXIOM

• • •

Mackerel sky and mare's tails
Make tall ships carry small sails.
——TRADITIONAL SEAMAN'S WEATHER AXIOM

• • •

Seagull, seagull, get out on the sand.
We'll ne'er have good weather with thee on hand.
——TRADITIONAL SEAMAN'S WEATHER AXIOM

• • •

Mugshut grey and dawn sky red,
Clap on your hat or you'll wet your head.
—TRADITIONAL SAILOR'S WEATHER AXIOM

• • •

Following the light of the sun, we left the Old World.
—CHRISTOPHER COLUMBUS

• • •

The bows glided down, and the coast
Blackened with birds took a last look
At his thrashing hair and whale-blue eye.
—DYLAN THOMAS
Ballad of the Long-Legged Bait

● ● ●

When the mist rolls o'er the land,
The rain comes pouring off the sand.
—TRADITIONAL SEAMAN'S WEATHER AXIOM

● ● ●

Red sky at morning, sailors take warning.
—TRADITIONAL SEAMAN'S WEATHER AXIOM

• • •

If red the Sun begins his race,
Be sure the rain will fall apace.
—TRADITIONAL SEAMAN'S WEATHER AXIOM

• • •

If wooly fleeces deck the heavenly way,
No rain will mar a summer's day.
—TRADITIONAL SEAMAN'S WEATHER AXIOM

• • •

Like a red morn that ever yet betokened,
Wreck to the seaman, tempest to the field.
—TRADITIONAL SEAMAN'S WEATHER AXIOM

• • •

A wind-gall at morn, fine weather all gone;
A rainbow at night, fine weather in sight.
—TRADITIONAL SEAMAN'S WEATHER AXIOM

• • •

Rainbow to windward, foul falls the day.
Rainbow to leeward, rain runs away.
—TRADITIONAL SEAMAN'S WEATHER AXIOM

● ● ●

A rainbow at night is a sailor's delight;
A bow in the morning—a sailor's warning.
—TRADITIONAL SEAMAN'S WEATHER AXIOM

● ● ●

When the sea-hog jumps, stand to your pumps.
——TRADITIONAL SEAMAN'S WEATHER AXIOM

● ● ●

We were all sea-swallow'd, though some cast again,
And by that destiny to perform an act
Whereof what's past is prologue, what to come
In yours and my discharge.
——WILLIAM SHAKESPEARE
The Tempest

● ● ●

Of a wind dog to windward beware,
For bad weather you must prepare
—TRADITIONAL SEAMAN'S WEATHER AXIOM

• • •

If clouds look as if scratched by a hen,
Get ready to reef your topsails then.
—TRADITIONAL SEAMAN'S WEATHER AXIOM

• • •

In that hour after dawn the horizon did not seem far away. The line where the watery sky met the grey sea was not well defined; it was as if the cheerless clouds grew denser out towards that circle until at the final meeting, all the way round, there was not an abrupt transition, but a simple mingling of the twin elements.

—C. S. FORESTER
The Good Shepherd

• • •

Comes the rain before the wind,
Then your sheets and halyards mind.
—TRADITIONAL SEAMAN'S WEATHER AXIOM

• • •

If the sun goes pale to bed,
'Twill rain tomorrow, so 'tis said.
—TRADITIONAL SEAMAN'S WEATHER AXIOM

• • •

The moon, the governess of the floods,
Pale in her anger, washes all the air.
—TRADITIONAL SEAMAN'S WEATHER AXIOM

• • •

When round the moon there is a brough (halo),
The weather comes in cold and rough.
—TRADITIONAL SEAMAN'S WEATHER AXIOM

• • •

The bigger the brough (halo), the bigger the breeze.
—TRADITIONAL SEAMAN'S WEATHER AXIOM

• • •

Long foretold, long last;
Short notice, soon past.
—TRADITIONAL SEAMAN'S WEATHER AXIOM

• • •

Weather-Eye

The hollow winds begin to blow,
The clouds look black and the glass is low;
Last night the sun went pale to bed,
The moon in haloes hid her head.
Look out, my lads! A wicked gale
With heavy rain will soon assail.
—TRADITIONAL SEAMAN'S WEATHER AXIOM

• • •

When rise commences after low,
Squalls expect and then clear blow.
—TRADITIONAL SEAMAN'S WEATHER AXIOM

• • •

A sharp rise after blow
Foretells a stronger blow.
—TRADITIONAL SEAMAN'S WEATHER AXIOM

• • •

Too fine to last.
—TRADITIONAL SEAMAN'S WEATHER AXIOM

• • •

The answer is to keep your eyes open all the time. If you can't
avoid a squall on your present tack then for Crissake change it,
and change it while you're still well clear. If you can aim for the
trailing edge of the squall then do so by all means, for there's
generally a good breeze there.
—TRISTAN JONES
(*on dealing with tropical squalls*)
Adrift

• • •

Weather-Eye

When the wind shifts against the sun,
Trust it not for back it will run.
—TRADITIONAL SEAMAN'S WEATHER AXIOM

• • •

I saw the moon late yestere'en
With the old moon in her arm;
And I fear, I fear, my master dear,
We shall have a deadly storm.
—TRADITIONAL SEAMAN'S WEATHER AXIOM

• • •

If fowls roll in t' sand,
Cover y'r head for rain be to hand.
If t' cockerel craws as ye're goin' to bed,
T' sun will rise with a watery head.
—TRADITIONAL SEAMAN'S WEATHER AXIOM

• • •

The Little Blue Book of **Sailing Wisdom**

Heavy dews in hot weather
Foretell fair weather.
—Traditional seaman's weather axiom

• • •

The great contention of the sea and skies
Parted our fellowship—but, hark! A sail!
—William Shakespeare
Othello

• • •

Weather-Eye

When mist takes to the open sea,
Fine weather, shipmate, it will be.

—TRADITIONAL SEAMAN'S WEATHER AXIOM

• • •

A mackerel sky:
Let all your kites fly.

—TRADITIONAL SEAMAN'S WEATHER AXIOM

• • •

Filled with the face of heaven, which from afar
Comes down upon the waters; all its hues,
From the rich sunset to the rising star,
Their magical variety diffuse:
And now they change: a paler shadow strews
Its mantle o'er the mountains; parting day
Dies like the dolphin, whom each pang imbues
With a new color as it gasps away,
The last still lovelist, till—'tis gone—and all is grey.

—LORD BYRON
Childe Harold

• • •

Sheets and braces are very dangerous things to handle in a gale of wind. Every movement of the rope must be closely watched with one vigilant eye, while the other must be looking out for washing seas. The slightest inattention to the belaying of a mainsheet while men are hanging on may mean that it breaks loose just as the men expect it to be fast, when away it goes, with awful suddenness and force, dragging them clean overboard before their instinctive grip can be let go. The slightest inattention to the seas may mean an equally fatal result. Not once, nor twice, but several times, a whole watch has been washed away from the fore-braces by some gigantic wave, and every single man in it been drowned.

—WILLIAM WOOD
All Afloat

• • •

He who lets the sea lull him into a sense of security is in very grave danger.

—HAMMOND INNES

• • •

Or feeling—, as the storm increases,
The love of terror nerve thy breast,
Didst venture to the coast:
To see the mighty war-ship leap
From wave to wave upon the deep,
Like chamois goat from steep to steep,
Till low in valley lost.

—ALLSTON

• • •

The particular violence of the sea had ceased. The waves came without snarling. The obligation of the man at the oars was to keep the boat headed so that the tilt of the rollers would not capsize her, and to preserve her from filling when the crests rushed past. The black waves were silent and hard to be seen in the darkness. Often one was almost upon the boat before the oarsman was aware.

—STEPHEN CRANE
The Open Boat

• • •

PART SIX

The Philosophic Sailor

There are some people the sea doesn't suit, who prefer the mountains or the plain.
—SAMUEL BECKETT
Molloy

• • •

To reach a port we must sail, sometimes with the wind, and sometimes against it. But we must not drift or lie at anchor.
—OLIVER WENDELL HOLMES

• • •

The one real crime at sea is the crime of indecision.

—ANONYMOUS

• • •

'Tis the set of the sails, and not the gales, that tell us the way
to go.

—ELLA WHEELER WILCOX

"The Winds of Fate"

• • •

The Philosophic Sailor

Never set sail on someone else's star.
——PROVERB

• • •

There is a poetry of sailing as old as the world.
——ANTOINE DE SAINTE-EXUPÉRY

• • •

Since I grew tired of the chase
And search, I learned to find;
And since the wind blows in my face,
I sail with every wind.
——FRIEDRICH NIETZSCHE
"My Happiness"

• • •

Experience is the best master, but his fees are considerable.
—ANONYMOUS

• • •

While most accounts of the battles fought on the so-called
fields of honor have from time immemorial been unreliable, the
pictorial representations of great naval engagements are without
exception figments of the imagination.
—W. G. SEBALD
The Rings of Saturn

• • •

Now in the fervid noon the smooth bright sea
Heaves slowly, for the wandering winds are dead
That stirred it into foam. The lonely ship
Rolls wearily, and idly flap the sails
Against the creaking masts. The lightest sound
Is lost not on the ear, and things minute
Attract the observant eye.
—SAMUEL RICHARDSON

• • •

The Philosophic Sailor

I had been six years at sea, but had only seen Melbourne and Sydney, very good places, charming places in their way—but Bankok!

—JOSEPH CONRAD
Youth, A Narrative

• • •

One hand for yourself—one for the ship.

—TRADITIONAL SAILOR'S ADAGE

• • •

I never saw a moor,
I never saw the sea;
Yet know I how the heather looks,
And what a wave must be.
I never spoke with God,
Nor visited in Heaven;
Yet certain am I of the spot,
As if a chart were given.

—EMILY DICKINSON

• • •

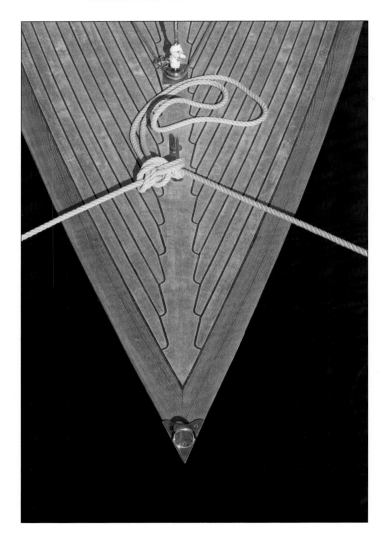

The Philosophic Sailor

You are not a fully fledged sailor unless you have sailed under
full sail.

—PROVERB

• • •

Salt beef, salt beef is our relief,
Salt beef and biscuit bread, oh!
Salt beef, salt beef is our relief,
Salt beef and biscuit bread, oh!
While you on shore and a great many more
On dainty dishes feed, oh!
Don't forget your old shipmate,
Fol-de-rol-de-riddle,
Fol-de-ri-do,
Our hammocks they swing wet and cold,
But in them we must lie, oh!
Our hammocks they swing wet and cold,
But in them we must lie, oh!
While you on shore, and a great many more,
Are sleeping warm and dry, oh!
Don't forget your old shipmate,
Fol-de-rol-de-riddle,
Fol-de-ri-do!

—TRADITIONAL SAILOR'S SONG, NINETEENTH CENTURY

• • •

One of the best temporary cures for pride and affectation that
I have ever seen tried is seasickness; a man who wants to vomit
never puts on airs.
—JOSH BILLINGS (HENRY WHEELER SHAW)
Josh Billings' Wit and Humor

• • •

Wide sea. That one continuous murmur breeds along the peb-
bled shore of memory!
—JOHN KEATS

• • •

We men and women are all in the same boat, upon a stormy sea.
We owe to each other a terrible and tragic loyalty.
—G. K. CHESTERTON
The Collected Works of G. K. Chesterton

• • •

We must free ourselves of the hope that the sea will ever rest. We must learn to sail in high winds.

—ARISTOTLE ONASSIS

● ● ●

Navigation is the art of moving a ship in *safety* from one place to another.

—COMMANDER JOHN IRVING
The Navigation of Small Yachts

● ● ●

I was shipwrecked before I got aboard.

—SENECA

● ● ●

Beware of your latter end.

——ADMIRAL TROUP

• • •

We are the boat, we are the sea, I sail in you, you sail in me.

——LORRIE WYATT

• • •

Fortune brings in some boats that are not steered.

——ANONYMOUS

• • •

For what avail the plow or sail,
Or land or life, if freedom fail?
—RALPH WALDO EMERSON
"Boston"

• • •

If you surrender to the wind, you can ride it.
—TONI MORRISON

• • •

It's an ill wind turns none to good.
—PROVERB

• • •

Any damn fool can circumnavigate the world sober. It takes a
really good sailor to do it drunk.
—SIR FRANCIS CHICHESTER

• • •

O Captain! my Captain! our fearful trip is done;
The ship has weather'd every rack, the prize we sought is won;
The port is near, the bells I hear, the people all exulting,
While follow eyes the steady keel, the vessel grim and daring:
But O heart! heart! heart!
Othe bleeding drops of red,
Where on the deck my Captain lies,
Fallen cold and dead.
—WALT WHITMAN

• • •

On life's vast ocean diversely we sail,
Reason the card, but passion is the gale.
—ALEXANDER POPE
"An Essay on Man"

• • •

O Captain! my Captain! rise up and hear the bells;
Rise up—for you the flag is flung—for you the bugle trills;
For you bouquets and ribbon'd wreaths—for you the shores
a-crowding;
For you they call, the swaying mass, their eager faces turning;
Here Captain! dear father!
This arm beneath your head;
—WALT WHITMAN

• • •

The person who goes farthest is generally the one who is willing to do and dare. The sure-thing boat never gets far from shore.
——DALE CARNEGIE

• • •

The pessimist complains about the wind; the optimist expects it to change; the realist adjusts the sails.
——WILLIAM A. WARD

• • •

At sea, I learned how little a person needs—not how much.
——ROBIN LEE GRAHAM

• • •

It is some dream that on the deck,
You've fallen cold and dead.
——WALT WHITMAN

• • •

Yes! Very funny this terrible thing is. A man that is born falls into a dream like a man who falls into the sea. If he tries to climb out into the air as inexperienced people endeavour to do, he drowns—*nicht wahr*? . . . No! I tell you! The way is to the destructive element submit yourself, and with the exertions of your hands and feet in the water make the deep, deep sea keep you up.

——JOSEPH CONRAD
Lord Jim

• • •

There were three Graces and three Muses—and there are three L's for the deep-sea sailor. Lead, Latitude, and Look-out; or Lead, Log, and Look-out. These still hold good, and in addition, the small-ship man must have three C's: Chart, Compass, and Confidence. And the greatest of these is Confidence.

——COMMANDER JOHN IRVING, RN
The Navigation of Small Yachts

• • •

Chiefly, the seashore has been the point of departure to knowledge, as to commerce. The most advanced nations are always those who have navigated the most.

——RALPH WALDO EMERSON
Society and Solitude

• • •

Why do you think my own racing yacht is named *Tenacious*, dummy? . . . Because I never quit. I've got a bunch of flags on my boat, but there ain't no white flags.

——TED TURNER

• • •

Give me this glorious ocean life, this salt-sea life, this briny, foamy life, when the sea neighs and snorts, and you breathe the very breath that the great whales respire! Let me roll around the globe, let me rock upon the sea; let me race and pant out my life with an eternal breeze astern, and an endless sea before!

——HERMAN MELVILLE
Redburn: His First Voyage

• • •

The Philosophic Sailor

The ocean has always been a salve to my soul—the best thing for a cut or abrasion was to go swimming in salt water. Later down the road of life, I made the discovery that salt water was also good for the mental abrasions one inevitably acquires on land.

—JIMMY BUFFETT

• • •

O My Soul, Your Voyages have been my Native Land.

—NIKOS KAZANTZAKIS

• • •

I remember my youth and the feeling that will never come back any more—the feeling that I could last forever, outlast the sea, the earth, and all men; the deceitful feeling that lures us on to joys, to perils, to love, to vain effort—to death; the triumphant conviction of strength, the heat of life in the handful of dust, the glow in the heart that with every year grows dim, grows cold, grows small, and expires, and expires too soon—before life itself.

—JOSEPH CONRAD
Youth, A Narrative

• • •

"Master, I marvel how the fishes live in the sea."
"Why, as men do a-land; the great ones eat up the little ones."
—THIRD AND FIRST FISHERMEN, WILLIAM SHAKESPEARE
Pericles, Prince of Tyre

• • •

The wind and the waves are always on the side of the ablest
navigator.
—EDWARD GIBBON

• • •

The Philosophic Sailor

Sailors, with their built in sense of order, service, and discipline,
should really be running the world.

—NICHOLAS MONSARRAT

• • •

The best of remedies is a beefsteak
Against sea-sickness; try it, Sir, before
You sneer, and I assure you this is true;
For I have found it answer—so may you.

—LORD BYRON
Don Juan

• • •

My Captain does not answer, his lips are pale and still;
My father does not feel my arm, he has no pulse nor will;
The ship is anchor'd safe and sound, its voyage closed and done;
From fearful trip, the victor ship, comes in with object won;
Exult, O shores, and ring, O bells!
But I, with mournful tread,
Walk the deck my Captain lies,
Fallen cold and dead.

—WALT WHITMAN
Leaves of Grass

• • •

There is nothing more enticing, disenchanting, and enslaving
than the life at sea.
——JOSEPH CONRAD

• • •

Now you take the brush,
And I'll take the pot,
And we'll paint the ship's side together.
When Jimmy comes along,
We'll sing a little song:
"Thank God we didn't join forever!"
——TRADITIONAL ROYAL NAVY SONG,
"Jimmy" is slang for a First Lieutenant

• • •

The Philosophic Sailor

I believe you can learn enough about sailing technique in one morning to set off on a voyage around the world that afternoon. I don't mean seamanship—the experience-honed judgment needed to handle a boat in all situations, which is the greatest requirement of the sailor—I mean the simple basic principles of how to move a boat with sails for any given wind. These principles are as follows: if the wind is from ahead, you pull the sails in; if the wind is from the side, you let them out a bit; if it's from behind, you let the sails way out. That's it.

—PETER NICHOLS
Sea Change: Alone Across the Atlantic in a Wooden Boat

• • •

Sleep, sleep, thou sad one, on the sea!
The wash of waters lull thee now;
His arm no more will pillow thee,
Thy hand upon his brow,
He is not near, to hurt thee, or to save:
The ground is his—the sea must be thy grave.

—RICHARD HENRY DANA
The Buccaneer

• • •

The fool hath his eye on the ends of the earth.
—ADMIRAL TROUP

• • •

My messmates, when ye drink my dirge,
Go, fill the cup from ocean's surge;
And when ye drain the beverage up,
Remember Neptune in the cup.
For he has been my *brawling host*,
Since first I roam'd from coast to coast;
And he my *brawling* host shall be—
I love his ocean courtesy—
His *boisterous* hospitality.
—GEORGE GRAY

• • •

The sea has neither meaning nor pity.
—ANTON CHEKHOV

• • •

"We have lost the first of the ebb," said the Director suddenly. I raised my head. The offing was barred by a black bank of clouds, and the tranquil waterway leading to the uttermost ends of the earth flowed somber under an overcast sky—seemed to lead into the heart of an immense darkness.

—JOSEPH CONRAD
Heart of Darkness

• • •

There is hope from the sea, but none from the grave.
—IRISH PROVERB

• • •

There are three sorts of people; those who are alive, those who are dead, and those who are at sea.
—ATTRIBUTED TO ANACHARSIS,
SIXTH CENTURY BC

• • •

The cure for anything is saltwater: sweat, tears, or the sea.
—ISAK DINESEN
The Deluge at Norderney

• • •

Some years ago—never mind how long precisely—having little or no money in my purse and nothing particular to interest me on shore, I thought I would sail about a little and see the watery part of the world.
—HERMAN MELVILLE
Moby Dick

• • •

"Wouldst thou,"—so the helmsman answered,
"Learn the secret of the sea?
Only those who brave its dangers
Comprehend its mystery!"
—HENRY WADSWORTH LONGFELLOW

• • •

The ebbs of tides and their mysterious flow,
We, as arts' elements shall understand,
And as by line upon the oceans go,
Whose paths shall be familiar as the land.

Instructed ships shall sail to quick commerce,
By which remotest regions are allied;
Which makes one city of the universe;
Where many gain, and all may be supplied.
—JOHN DRYDEN
"Annus Mirabilis"

• • •

Mackerel skies and mares tails, soon will be time to shorten sails.
—SAILOR'S PROVERB

• • •

We have ploughed the vast ocean in a fragile ship.
——OVID

• • •

It's like having an old wife. A devil you know is sometimes better than the devil you don't. At least we know we've got a good boat.
——TED TURNER, ON HAVING AN OLD BOAT

• • •

Men in a ship are always looking up, and men ashore are usually looking down.
——JOHN MASEFIELD

• • •

A small craft in an ocean is, or should be, a benevolent dictatorship.
——TRISTAN JONES

• • •

As usual I finish the day before the sea, sumptuous this evening beneath the moon, which writes Arab symbols with phosphorescent streaks on the slow swells. There is no end to the sky and waters. How well they accompany sadness.
——ALBERT CAMUS

• • •

He that will not sail till all dangers are over must never put to sea.
—THOMAS FULLER

• • •

Off Cape Horn there are but two kinds of weather—neither one
of them a pleasant kind.
—JOHN MASEFIELD

• • •

A sailor is an artist whose medium is the wind.
—WEBB CHILES

• • •

They who plough the sea do not carry the wind in their hands.
——SYRUS

• • •

For one thing, I was no longer alone; a man is never alone with
the wind—and the boat made three.
——HILAIRE BELLOC
Hills and the Sea

• • •

Ports are no good—ships rot, men go to the devil!
——JOSEPH CONRAD
The Mirror of the Sea

• • •

It isn't that life ashore is distasteful to me. But life at sea is better.
—SIR FRANCIS DRAKE

• • •

Oh! 'tis a thought sublime, that man can force
A path upon the waste, can find a way
Where all is trackless, and compel the winds,
Those freest agents of Almighty's power,
To lend their untamed wings, and bear him on
To distant climes.
—HENRY WARE

• • •

He who lets the sea lull him into a sense of security is in very
grave danger.
—HAMMOND INNES

• • •

The Philosophic Sailor

It's out there at sea that you are really yourself.
——VITO DUMAS

• • •

The art of the sailor is to leave nothing to chance.
——ANNIE VAN DE WIELE

• • •

Live in the sunshine, swim in the sea, drink the wild air.
——RALPH WALDO EMERSON

• • •

Whenever your preparations for the sea are poor, the sea worms
its way in and finds the problems.
—FRANCIS STOKES

• • •

Every drop in the sea counts.
—YOKO ONO

• • •

When a man comes to like a sea life, he is not fit to live on land.
—DR. SAMUEL JOHNSON

• • •

All the best cruises are planned the night before.
—COMMANDER JOHN IRVING
Cruising and Ocean Racing

• • •

Bad cooking is responsible for more trouble at sea than all other things put together.

——THOMAS FLEMING DAY

• • •

What makes mankind tragic is not that they are the victims of nature—it is that they are conscious of it.

——JOSEPH CONRAD
Collected Letters of Joseph Conrad

• • •

Years from now you will be more disappointed by the things that you didn't do than by the ones you did do. So throw off the bowlines. Sail away from the safe harbor. Catch the trade winds in your sails. Explore. Dream. Discover.

——MARK TWAIN

• • •

A lot of people ask me if I were shipwrecked, and could only have one book, what would it be? I always say, *How to Build a Boat.*
——STEPHEN WRIGHT

• • •

There is nothing like lying flat on your back on the deck, alone except for the helmsman aft at the wheel, silence except for the lapping of the sea against the side of the ship. At that time you can be equal to Ulysses and brother to him.
——ERROL FLYNN

• • •

The chance for mistakes is about equal to the number of crew squared.
——TED TURNER

• • •

The Philosophic Sailor

The days pass happily with me wherever my ship sails.
—CAPTAIN JOSHUA SLOCUM
Sailing Alone Around the World

• • •

Men may change their climate, but they cannot change their nature. A man that goes out a fool cannot ride or sail himself into common sense.
—JOSEPH ADDISON
The Tattler

• • •

Sailors ordinarily receive wrecked mariners kindly.
——JAMES FENIMORE COOPER
Afloat and Ashore

• • •

Back into the forecastle we cleaned house, washing out the dead man's bunk and removing every vestige of him. By sea law and sea custom, we should have gathered his effects together and turned them over to the captain, who, later, would have held an auction in which we should have bid for the various articles. But no man wanted them, so we tossed them up on deck and overboard in the wake of the departed body—the last ill-treatment we could devise to wreak upon the one we had hated so. Oh, it was raw, believe me; but the life we lived was raw, and we were as raw as the life.
——JACK LONDON
That Dead Men Rise Up Never

• • •

"I only remember one part of the service," he said, "and that is 'And the body shall be cast into the sea'. So cast it in."
—JACK LONDON / CAPT. WOLF LARSEN
The Sea Wolf

• • •

Surgeon: You'll lose more . . . if you don't put ashore for fresh food and water!
Captain Hornblower: Perhaps you'll dig into your medical kit and get me a breath of fresh wind.
—C. S. FORESTER
Captain Hornblower (film)

• • •

Shipwrecks are—a propos—of nothing. If men could only train for them and have them occur when the men had reached pink condition, there would be less drowning at sea.
—STEPHEN CRANE
The Open Boat

• • •

"Well," continued the captain, "you know, at all events, that there's salt in the sea, and I may tell you that there is lime also, besides other things. At the equator, the heat bein' great, water is evaporated faster than anywhere else, so that there the sea is salter and has more lime in it than elsewhere. Besides that it is hotter. Of course, that being the case, its weight is different from the waters of the cold polar seas, so it is bound to move away an' get itself freshened and cooled. In like manner, the cold water round the poles feels obliged to flow to the equator to get itself salted and warmed. This state of things, as a natural consequence, causes commotion in the sea. The commotion is moreover increased by the millions of shell-fish that dwell there. These creatures, not satisfied with their natural skins, must needs have shells on their backs, and they extract lime from the sea-water for the purpose of makin' these shells. This process is called secretin' the lime; coral insects do the same, and, as many of the islands of the south seas are made by coral insects, you may guess that a considerable lot of lime is made away with. The commotion or disturbance thus created produces two great currents—from the equator to the poles and from the poles to the equator. But there are many little odds and ends about the world that affect and modify these currents, such as depth, and local heat and cold, and rivers and icebergs, but the chief modifiers are continents. The currents flowin' north from the Indian Ocean and southern seas rush up between Africa and America. The space bein' narrow—comparatively—they form one strong current, on doublin' the Cape of Good Hope, which flies right across to the Gulf of Mexico. Here it is turned aside and flows in a nor'-easterly direction, across the Atlantic towards England and Norway, under the name of the Gulf Stream, but the Gulf of Mexico has no more to do with it than the man in the moon, 'xcept in the way of turnin' it out of its nat'ral course. This Gulf Stream is a *river of warm water* flowing through the cold waters of the Atlantic; it keeps separate, and wherever it flows the climate is softened. It embraces Ireland, and makes the climate there so mild that there is, as you know, scarcely any frost all the year round—"

—R. M. BALLANTYNE

Sunk at Sea

• • •

The Philosophic Sailor

An angry skipper makes an unhappy crew.
——RUDYARD KIPLING
Captains Courageous

• • •

The clouds were building up now for the trade wind and he
looked ahead and saw a flight of wild ducks etching themselves
against the sky over the water, then blurring, then etching again
and he knew no man was ever alone on the sea.
——ERNEST HEMINGWAY
The Old Man and the Sea

• • •

No pessimist ever discovered the secret of the stars or sailed to an
uncharted land, or opened a new doorway for the human spirit.
——HELEN KELLER

• • •

If we who have sailed together
Flit out of each other's view,
The world will sail on, I think,
Just as it used to do.
—WILL CARLETON

● ● ●

Rest after toil.
Port after stormy seas.
Death after life.
These things do greatly please.
—ANONYMOUS

● ● ●

PART SEVEN

Sea-Fever

I must go down to the sea again, to the lonely sea and sky,
And all I ask is a tall ship and a star to steer her by.
—JOHN MASEFIELD
"Sea Fever"

• • •

To young men contemplating a voyage I would say go.
—CAPTAIN JOSHUA SLOCUM
Sailing Alone Around the World

• • •

The sun is shining on the sea,
Shining with all its might:
He did his best to make
The billows smooth and bright—
And this was very odd, because it was
The middle of the night.
—LEWIS CARROLL
"The Walrus and the Carpenter"

• • •

I bit my arm, I sucked the blood,
And cried, A sail! a sail!
—SAMUEL TAYLOR COLERIDGE
The Rime of the Ancient Mariner

• • •

Sea-Fever

Sunset and evening star,
And one clear call for me!
And may there be no moaning of the bar,
When I put out to sea,

But such a tide as moving seems asleep,
Too full for sound and foam,
When that which drew from out the boundless deep
Turns again home.

Twilight and evening bell,
And after that the dark!
And may there be no sadness of farewell,
When I embark;

For tho' from out our bourne of Time and Place
The flood may bear me far,
I hope to see my Pilot face to face
When I have crossed the bar.
—LORD ALFRED TENNYSON
"Crossing the Bar"

● ● ●

On life's vast ocean diversely we sail. Reasons the card, but passion the gale.
——ALEXANDER POPE

• • •

A sailor's joys are as simple as a child's.
——BERNARD MOITESSIER
The Long Way

• • •

Now I would give a thousand furlongs of sea for an acre of barren ground.
——WILLIAM SHAKESPEARE
The Tempest

• • •

Worth seeing? Yes; but not worth going to sea.
——DR. SAMUEL JOHNSON
Life of Samuel Johnson

• • •

The sea pronounces something, over and over, in a hoarse
whisper; I cannot quite make it out.
——ANNIE DILLARD
Teaching a Stone to Talk: Expeditions and Encounters

• • •

The bows glided down
But more wonderful than the lore of old men and the lore of
books is the secret of the ocean.
—H. P. LOVECRAFT

• • •

Though inland far we be,
Our souls have sight of that immortal sea
Which brought us hither.
——WILLIAM WORDSWORTH
"Ode: Intimations of Immortality"

• • •

To be truly challenging, a voyage, like a life, must rest on a firm
foundation of financial unrest.
——STERLING HAYDEN
Wanderer

• • •

Overhead, the white sails stretched their arms to catch the night
wind. They were my sails—my wings—and they brought me to
the sea of my boyhood dreams.
——WILLIAM ROBINSON
10,000 Leagues Over the Sea

• • •

Sea-Fever

The voyage was to be round the world, and it took my fancy
at the very sound. The ship was to take a cargo of flour to
England; there, she was to receive a small assorted cargo for the
North-West Coast, and some of the sandal-wood islands;
after disposing of her toys and manufactures in barter, she was
to sail for Canton, exchange her furs, wood and other articles for
teas, &c., and return home.
—JAMES FENIMORE COOPER
Afloat and Ashore

• • •

God moves in a mysterious way, his wonders to perform.
He plants his footsteps in the seas, and rides upon the storm.
—WILLIAM COWPER

• • •

. . . the chief-mate resorting to some brandy in order to prevent
his taking cold. On what principle this is done, I cannot explain,
though I know it is often practised, and in all quarters
of the world.
—JAMES FENIMORE COOPER
Afloat and Ashore

• • •

Sea-Fever

A man can sail in the forecastles of big ships all his life and
never know what real sailing is. From the time I was twelve,
I listened to the lure of the sea. When I was fifteen I was captain
and owner of an oyster-pirate sloop. By the time I was sixteen
I was sailing in scow-schooners, fishing salmon with the Greeks
up the Sacramento River, and serving as sailor on the Fish Patrol.
And I was a good sailor, too, though all my cruising had been on
San Francisco Bay and the rivers tributary to it. I had never been
on the ocean in my life.

—JACK LONDON
The Human Drift

• • •

White as a white sail on a dusky sea,
When half the island's clouded and half free,
Fluttering between the dun wave and the sky,
Is hope's last gleam in man's extremity.

—LORD BYRON
The Island

• • •

Appendix

RULES OF THE ROAD FOR POWERED VESSELS
(Rendered in verse to aid memory)

1. Two Powered Vessels Meeting

When both lights you see ahead,
Starboard wheel and show your Red.

2. Two Powered Vessels Passing

Green to Green—or Red to Red
Perfect safety—go ahead.

3. Two Powered Vessels Crossing

If to your Starboard Red appear
It is your duty to keep clear;
To act as judgment says is proper,
To Port—or Starboard—Back—or stop her.

But when upon your Port is seen
A Steamer's Starboard Light of Green,

Appendix

There's not so much for you to do,
For Green to Port keeps clear of you.

4.   All Ships must keep a look-out, and Powered Vessels must
     Stop and go Astern if necessary.

Both in safety and in doubt
Always keep a good look-out;
In danger with no room to turn,
Ease her—Stop her—go Astern.

RULES OF THE ROAD FOR SAILING VESSELS

A close-hauled ship you'll NEVER see
Give way to one that's running free.
It's easier running free to steer
And that's the reason she keeps clear.

With wind the same side, running free,
One's to Windward, one's to Lee.
The Leeward ship goes straight ahead,
The other alters course instead.

Both "close-hauled" or both quite "free"
On DIFFERENT TACKS, we all agree,
The ship that has the wind to PORT
Must keep well clear, is what we're taught.
At other times, the altering craft
Is that which has the wind right aft.

A Sailor's Glossary

By Richard Henry Dana

Aback   The situation of the sails when the wind presses their surfaces against the mast, and tends to force the vessel astern.

Abaft   Toward the stern of a vessel.

Ahead   In the direction of the vessel's head. *Wind ahead* is from the direction toward which the vessel's head points.

A-hull   The situation of a vessel when she lies with all her sails furled and her helm lashed a-lee.

A-lee   The situation of the helm when it is put in the opposite direction from that in which the wind blows.

All-aback   When all the sails are aback.

Avast, or 'Vast An order to stop; as, "Avast heaving!"

A-weather   The situation of the helm when it is put in the direction from which the wind blows.

A Sailor's Glossary

Back
To back an anchor, is to carry out a smaller one ahead of the one by which the vessel rides, to take off some of the strain.

To back a sail, is to throw it aback.

To back and fill, is alternately to back and fill the sails.

Backstays
Stays running from a masthead to the vessel's side, slanting a little aft.

Bark, or Barque
A three-masted vessel, having her fore and main masts rigged like a ship's, and her mizzen mast like the main mast of a schooner, with no sail upon it but a spanker, and gaff topsail.

Bearing
The direction of an object from the person looking. The *bearings* of a vessel, are the widest part of her below the plank-shear. That part of her hull which is on the water-line when she is at anchor and in her proper trim.

Beating
Going toward the direction of the wind, by alternate tacks.

Bend
To make fast.

Boom
A spar used to extend the foot of a fore-and-aft sail or studdingsail.

Bound
Wind-bound. When a vessel is kept in port by a head wind.

Bow
The rounded part of a vessel, forward.

Bower A working anchor, the cable of which is bent and reeved through the hawse-hole.

Bowsprit (Pronounced bo-sprit.) A large and strong spar, standing from the bows of a vessel.

Box-hauling Wearing a vessel by backing the head sails.

Box *To box the compass*, is to repeat the thirty-two points of the compass in order.

Brace A rope by which a yard is turned about.

To brace a yard, is to turn it about horizontally.

To brace up, is to lay the yard more fore-and-aft.

To brace in, is to lay it nearer square.

To brace aback.

To brace to, is to brace the head yards a little aback, in tacking or wearing.

Brig A square-rigged vessel, with two masts. An *hermaphrodite brig* has a brig's foremast and a schooner's mainmast.

Broach-to To fall off so much, when going free, as to bring the wind round on the other quarter and take the sails aback.

Buntlines Ropes used for hauling up the body of a sail.

By *By the head.* Said of a vessel when her head is lower in the water than her stern. If her stern is lower, she is *by the stern.*

Carry-away   To break a spar, or part a rope.

Cast   To pay a vessel's head off, in getting under way, on the tack she is to sail upon.

Close-hauled   Applied to a vessel which is sailing with her yards braced up so as to get as much as possible to windward. The same as *on a taut bowline, full and by, on the wind*, &c.

Courses   The common term for the sails that hang from a ship's lower yards. The foresail is called the *fore course* and the mainsail the *main course.*

Cuddy   A cabin in the fore part of a boat.

Cutter   A small boat. Also, a kind of sloop.

Dead Reckoning   A reckoning kept by observing a vessel's courses and distances by the log, to ascertain her position.

Even-keel   The situation of a vessel when she is so trimmed that she sits evenly upon the water, neither end being down more than the other.

Fag   A rope is *fagged* when the end is untwisted.

Fathom   Six feet.

Flat   A sheet is said to be hauled *flat*, when it is hauled down close.

Flat-aback, when a sail is blown with its after surface against the mast.

Fore Used to distinguish the forward part of a vessel, or things in that direction; as, *fore mast, fore hatch*, in opposition to *aft* or *after*.

Fore-and-aft Lengthwise with the vessel. In opposition to *athwart-ships*.

Fore Mast The forward mast of all vessels.

Founder A vessel *founders*, when she fills with water and sinks.

Full-and-by Sailing close-hauled on a wind.

Full-and-by! The order given to the man at the helm to keep the sails full and at the same time close to the wind.

Furl To roll a sail up snugly on a yard or boom, and secure it.

Gaff A spar, to which the head of a fore-and-aft sail is bent.

Gaff-topsail A light sail set over a gaff, the foot being spread by it.

Galley The place where the cooking is done.

Haul *Haul her wind*, said of a vessel when she comes up close upon the wind.

A Sailor's Glossary

Head-sails	A general name given to all sails that set forward of the fore-mast.
Irons	A ship is said to be *in irons*, when, in working, she will not cast one way or the other.
Jib	A triangular sail set on a stay, forward.
	Flying-jib sets outside of the jib; and the *jib-o'-jib* outside of that.
Jib-boom	The boom, rigged out beyond the bowsprit, to which the tack of the jib is lashed.
Kedge	A small anchor, with an iron stock, used for warping.
	To kedge, is to warp a vessel ahead by a kedge and hawser.
Larboard	The left side of a vessel, looking forward.
Lee	The side opposite to that from which the wind blows; as, if a vessel has the wind on her starboard side, that will be the *weather*, and the larboard will be the *lee* side.
	A lee shore is the shore upon which the wind is blowing.

Under the lee of anything, is when you have that between you and the wind.

By the lee. The situation of a vessel, going free, when she has fallen off so much as to bring

the wind round her stern, and to take her sails aback on the other side.

Leeward
(Pronounced *lu-ard***)** The lee side. In a direction opposite to that from which the wind blows, which is called *windward.* The opposite of *lee* is *weather,* and of *leeward* is *windward*; the two first being adjectives.

Lie-to, is to stop the progress of a vessel at sea, either by counter-bracing the yards, or by reducing sail so that she will make little or no headway, but will merely come to and fall off by the counteraction of the sails and helm.

List The inclination of a vessel to one side; as, a *list* to port, or a *list* to starboard.

Lubber's Hole A hole in the top, next the mast.

Luff To put the helm so as to bring the ship up nearer to the wind. *Spring-a-luff! Keep your luff!* &c. Orders to luff. Also, the roundest part of a vessel's bow. Also, the forward leech of fore-and-aft sails.

Lugger A small vessel carrying lug-sails.

Lug-sail A sail used in boats and small vessels, bent to a yard which hangs obliquely to the mast.

A Sailor's Glossary

Man-ropes   Ropes used in going up and down a vessel's side.

Mast   A spar set upright from the deck, to support rigging, yards and sails. Masts are whole or *made*.

Miss-stays   To fail of going about from one tack to another.

Mizzen-mast   The aftermost mast of a ship. The spanker is sometimes called the *mizzen*.

Moor   To secure by two anchors.

Offing   Distance from the shore.

Orlop   The lower deck of a ship of the line; or that on which the cables are stowed.

Out-rigger   A spar rigged out to windward from the tops or cross-trees, to spread the breast-backstays.

Painter   A rope attached to the bows of a boat, used for making her fast.

Pay-off   When a vessel's head falls off from the wind.

Port   Used instead of *larboard*.

To port the helm, is to put it to the larboard.

Port, or Port-hole   Holes in the side of a vessel, to point cannon out of. (See Bridle.)

Puddening   A quantity of yarns, matting or oakum, used to prevent chafing.

Quarter   The part of a vessel's side between the after part of the main chains and the stern. The *quarter* of a yard is between the slings and the yard-arm.

The wind is said to be *quartering*, when it blows in a line between that of the keel and the beam and abaft the latter.

Rake   The inclination of a mast from the perpendicular.

Ratlines (Pronounced *rat-lins*)   Lines running across the shrouds, horizontally, like the rounds of a ladder, and used to step upon in going aloft.

Reef   To reduce a sail by taking in upon its head, if a square sail, and its foot, if a fore-and-aft sail.

A *reef* is all of the sail that is comprehended between the head of the sail and the first reef-band, or between two reef-bands.

Reeve   To pass the end of a rope through a block, or any aperture.

Rigging   The general term for all the ropes of a vessel.

Also, the common term for the shrouds with their ratlines; as, the *main rigging, mizzen rigging*, &c.

Road, or Roadstead   An anchorage at some distance from the shore.

Rolling Tackle   Tackles used to steady the yards in a heavy sea.

Royal A light sail next above a topgallant sail.

Royal Yard The yard from which the royal is set. The fourth from the deck.

Rudder The machine by which a vessel or boat is steered.

Runner A rope used to increase the power of a tackle. It is rove through a single block which you wish to bring down, and a tackle is hooked to each end, or to one end, the other being made fast.

Running Rigging The ropes that reeve through blocks, and are pulled and hauled, such as braces, halyards, &c.; in opposition to the *standing rigging*, the ends of which are securely seized, such as stays, shrouds, &c.

Sails are of two kinds: *square sails*, which hang from yards, their foot lying across the line of the keel, as the courses, topsails, &c.; and *fore-and-aft sails*, which set upon gaffs, or on stays, their foot running with the line of the keel, as jib, spanker, &c.

Schooner A small vessel with two masts and no tops.

A *fore-and-aft schooner* has only fore-and-aft sails.

A *topsail schooner* carries a square fore topsail, and frequently, also, topgallant sail and royal. There are some schooners with three masts. They also have no tops.

A *main-topsail schooner* is one that carries square topsails, fore and aft.

Score   A groove in a block or dead-eye.

Scotchman   A large batten placed over the turnings-in of rigging.

Scud   To drive before a gale, with no sail, or only enough to keep the vessel ahead of the sea. Also, low, thin clouds that fly swiftly before the wind.

Scuppers   Holes cut in the water-ways for the water to run from the decks.

Scuttle   A hole cut in a vessel's deck, as, a hatchway. Also, a hole cut in any part of a vessel.

To scuttle, is to cut or bore holes in a vessel to make her sink.

Sheet   A rope used in setting a sail, to keep the clew down to its place. With square sails, the sheets run through each yard-arm. With boom sails,

they haul the boom over one way and another. They keep down the inner clew of a studdingsail and the after clew of a jib.

Sheet Anchor   A vessel's largest anchor: not carried at the bow.

Shrouds   A set of ropes reaching from the mast-heads to the vessel's sides, to support the masts.

Skysail   A light sail next above the royal.

Sky-scraper   A name given to a *skysail* when it is triangular.

Slings   The ropes used for securing the centre of a yard to the mast.

     Yard-slings are now made of iron. Also, a large rope fitted so as to go round any article which is to be hoisted or lowered.

Slip   To let a cable go and stand out to sea.

     Slip-rope. A rope bent to the cable just outside the hawse-hole, and brought in on the weather quarter, for slipping.

Sloop   A small vessel with one mast.

Spanker   The after sail of a ship or bark. It is a fore-and-aft sail, setting with a boom and gaff.

Spar   The general term for all masts, yards, booms, gaffs, &c.

Spill   To shake the wind out of a sail by bracing it so that the wind may strike its leech and shiver it.

Splice   To join two ropes together by interweaving their strands.

Spoon-drift   Water swept from the tops of the waves by the violence of the wind in a tempest, and driven along before it, covering the surface of the sea.

Sprit   A small boom or gaff, used with some sails in small boats. The lower end rests in a becket or snotter by the foot of the mast, and the other end spreads and raises the outer upper corner of the sail, crossing it diagonally. A sail so rigged in a boat is called a *sprit-sail*.

Sprit-sail-yard   A yard lashed across the bowsprit or knight-heads, and used to spread the guys of the jib and flying jib-boom. There was formerly a sail bent to it called a *sprit-sail*.

Standing Rigging   That part of a vessel's rigging which is made fast and not hauled upon.

Starboard   The right side of a vessel, looking forward.

Stay   To tack a vessel, or put her about, so that the wind, from being on one side, is brought upon the other, round the vessel's head.

To stay a mast, is to incline it forward or aft, or to one side or the other, by the stays and back-stays. Thus, a mast is said to be *stayed* too much forward or aft, or too much to port, &c.

Stays. Large ropes, used to support masts, and leading from the head of some mast down to some other mast, or to some part of the vessel. Those which lead forward are called *fore-and-aft stays*; and those which lead down to the vessel's sides, *backstays*.

In stays, or *hove in stays*, the situation of a vessel when she is *staying*, or going about from one tack to the other.

A Sailor's Glossary

Staysail   A sail which hoists upon a stay.

Steady!   An order to keep the helm as it is.

Steerage   That part of the between-decks which is just forward of the cabin.

Step   A block of wood secured to the keel, into which the heel of the mast is placed.

To step a mast, is to put it in its step.

Stern   The after end of a vessel.

Stiff   The quality of a vessel which enables it to carry a great deal of sail without lying over much on her side. The opposite to *crank*.

Tack   To put a ship about, so that from having the wind on one side, you bring it round on the other by the way of her head. The opposite of *wearing*.

A vessel is on the *starboard tack*, or has her *starboard tacks on board*, when she has the wind on her starboard side.

Tackle (Pronounced tay-cle)   A purchase, formed by a rope rove through one or more blocks.

Tail   A rope spliced into the end of a block and used for making it fast to rigging or spars. Such a block is called a *tail-block*.

A ship is said to *tail* up or down stream, when at anchor, according as her stern swings up or down with the tide; in opposition to *heading* one way or another, which is said of a vessel when under way.

Tarpaulin
A piece of canvass, covered with tar, used for covering hatches, boats, &c. Also, the name commonly given to a sailor's hat when made of tarred or painted cloth.

Tide
To *tide up or down* a river or harbor, is to work up or down with a fair tide and head wind or calm, coming to anchor when the tide turns.

Tide-rode
The situation of a vessel, at anchor, when she swings by the force of the tide. In opposition to *wind-rode.*

Tiller
A bar of wood or iron, put into the head of the rudder, by which the rudder is moved.

Timenoguy
A rope carried taut between different parts of the vessel, to prevent the sheet or tack of a course from getting foul, in working ship.

Top
A platform, placed over the head of a lower mast, resting on the trestle-trees, to spread the rigging, and for the convenience of men aloft.

To *top* up a yard or boom, is to raise up one end of it by hoisting on the lift.

Top-block. A large iron-bound block, hooked into a bolt under the lower cap, and used for the top-rope to reeve through in sending up and down topmasts.

Topmast
The second mast above the deck. Next above the lower mast.

Topgallant Mast
The third mast above the deck.

Top-rope
The rope used for sending topmasts up and down.

Topsail
The second sail above the deck.

Topgallant Sail
The third sail above the deck.

Tow
To draw a vessel along by means of a rope.

Traveller
An iron ring, fitted so as to slip up and down a rope.

Trice
To haul up by means of a rope.

Trick
The time allotted to a man to stand at the helm.

Trim
The condition of a vessel, with reference to her cargo and ballast. A vessel is *trimmed* by the head or by the stern.

In ballast trim, is when she has only ballast on board.

Also, to arrange the sails by the braces with reference to the wind.

Truck   A circular piece of wood, placed at the head of the highest mast on a ship. It has small holes or sheaves in it for signal halyards to be rove through. Also, the wheel of a gun-carriage.

Truss   The rope by which the centre of a lower yard is kept in toward the mast.

Trysail   A fore-and-aft sail, set with a boom and gaff, and hoisting on a small mast abaft the lower mast, called a *trysail-mast*. This name is generally confined to the sail so carried at the mainmast of a full-rigged brig; those carried at the foremast and at the mainmast of a ship or bark being called *spencers*, and those that are at the mizzenmast of a ship or bark, *spankers*.

Unbend   To cast off or untie.

Union   The upper inner corner of an ensign. The rest of the flag is called the *fly*. The *union* of the U.S. ensign is a blue field with white stars, and the *fly* is composed of alternate white and red stripes.

              Union-down. The situation of a flag when it is hoisted upside down, bringing the union down instead of up. Used as a signal of distress.

Vane
A fly worn at the mast-head, made of feathers or buntine, traversing on a spindle, to show the direction of the wind.

Waist
That part of the upper deck between the quarter-deck and forecastle.

Waisters. Green hands, or broken-down seamen, placed in the waist of a man-of-war.

Wake
The track or path a ship leaves behind her in the water.

Wall-sided
A vessel is *wall-sided* when her sides run up perpendicularly from the bends. In opposition to *tumbling-home* or *flaring out.*

Ware, or Wear
To turn a vessel round, so that, from having the wind on one side, you bring it upon the other, carrying her stern round by the wind. In *tacking,* the same result is produced by carrying a vessel's head round by the wind.

Warp
To move a vessel from one place to another by means of a rope made fast to some fixed object, or to a kedge.

Anchor watch, a small watch of one or two men, kept while in port.

Weather gage. A vessel has the *weather gage* of another when she is to windward of her.

A *weatherly ship*, is one that works well to windward, making but little leeway.

Weather Roll   The roll which a ship makes to windward.

Weigh   To lift up; as, to weigh an anchor or a mast.

Wheel   The instrument by which a ship is steered; being a barrel, (round which the tiller-ropes go,) and a wheel with spokes.

Winch   A purchase formed by a horizontal spindle or shaft with a wheel or crank at the end. A small one with a wheel is used for making ropes or spunyarn.

Windlass   The machine used in vessels to weigh the anchor by.

Wing-and-wing   The situation of a fore-and-aft vessel when she is going dead before the wind, with her foresail hauled over on one side and her mainsail on the other.

Withe, or Wythe   An iron instrument fitted on the end of a boom or mast, with a ring to it, through which another boom or mast is rigged out and secured.

Wring   To bend or strain a mast by setting the rigging up too taut.

A Sailor's Glossary

Yacht   A vessel of pleasure or state.

Yard   A long piece of timber, tapering slightly toward the ends, and hung by the centre to a mast, to spread the square sails upon.

Yard-arm   The extremities of a yard.

Yaw   The motion of a vessel when she goes off from her course.

INDEX

A

Addison, Joseph, 169

Adrift, 128

Afloat and Ashore, 78, 110, 112, 170, 182-183

Alcott, Louisa May, 83

Allston, 133

American Folk Song, 95

Anacharsis, 157

"An Essay on Man," 146

"Annus Mirabilis," 159

Aran Islands, The, 19

Ars Amatoria, 44

Atkinson, Brooks, 64

B

Ballad of the Long-Legged Bait, 117

Ballantyne, R. M., 80, 172

Bamford, Don, 88

Battleship Potemkin, 82

Beckett, Samuel, 134

Beiser, Arthur, 63

Belloc, Hilaire, 71, 163

Beowulf, 35, 56–57, 60

Bierce, Ambrose, 14

Billings, Josh (Henry Wheeler Shaw), 142

"Blow, Bully Boys, Blow," 70

Blue Posts Inn, 61

"Boston," 145

Brainard, 46

Brennan, Stephen Vincent, ix, 16, 25, 106

Breton Fisherman's Prayer, 74

Broke, Captain Philip, 53

Buccaneer, The, 155

Buffett, Jimmy, 151

Building a Little Ship, 73

Burney, W., 57

INDEX

Byron, Lord, 13, 20, 49, 131, 153, 185

C

Calvin, John, 104
Camus, Albert, 161
Canto I, 59
Carleton, Will, 174
Carnegie, Dale, 148
Carroll, Lewis, 176
Carvel, Paul, 17
Chapman, George, 36, 52
Chekhov, Anton, 156
Chesterton, G. K., 142
Chichester, Sir Francis, 145
Childe Harold, 131
Chiles, Webb, 162
Churchill, Winston, 38
Coleridge, Samuel Taylor, 11, 17, 29, 72, 76, 101, 176
Collected Letters of Joseph Conrad, 167
Collected Works of G. K. Chesterton, The, 142
Columbus, Christopher, 116
Connor, Dennis, 71
Conrad, Joseph, 2, 8, 10, 13, 21, 37, 39, 51, 64, 87, 101, 104-105, 139, 149, 151, 154, 157, 163, 167
Cooper, James Fenimore, 78, 110, 112, 170, 183-184

Cousteau, Jacques-Yves, 10
Cowper, William, 184
Crane, Stephen, 46, 111, 133, 171
Cruise of the "Nona," The, 71
Cruising and Ocean Racing, 166
"Crossing the Bar," 177
Culler, R. D., 69
Cummings, E. E., 4
Cunningham, Allan, 76
Curtis, George William, 73

D

Dana, Richard Henry, 26, 155, 188-207
Dampier, William, 85
Davis, Charles G., 92
Day, Thomas Fleming, 167
Deep Water Cruising, 18
Deluge at Norderney, The, 158
Dibdin, Charles, 47
Diary of Samuel Pepys: 1665, The, 84
Dickinson, Emily, 32, 139
Dillard, Annie, 179
Dinesen, Isak, 42, 158
"Don Juan," 153
Donleavy, J. P., 93
Donne, John, 83, 92, 96, 102
Douglas Service, 58
Drake, Sir Francis, 164
Dryden, John, 159
Dumas, Vito, 165

E
Eisenstein, Sergi, 82
Emerson, Ralph Waldo, 145, 150,
    165
Epode, 11

F
Falconer, William, 91
Finnish Sailing Proverb, 4
*First Salute: A View of the Amer-
    ican Revolution*, 58
*Flight of the "Firecrest,"
    The*, 97
Flynn, Errol, 168
Forester, C. S., 47, 124, 171
French Proverb, 21
Fuller, Thomas, 162

G
Gandhi, Mahatma, 14
Gann, Ernest K., 50
Gay, John, 46
*Generation of Swine: Tales of
    Shame and Degredation in the
    '80s*, 5
Gerbault, Alain, 97
Gibbon, Edward, 152
Gibbons, Thomas, 54
Gilbert, Sir Humphrey, 1
Gilbert, W. S., 45
Good Shepherd, The, 124
Graham, Robin Lee, 148

Grahame, Kenneth, 77
Graves, Robert, 43
Gray, George, 156

H
Hamilton, Donald, 94
Hayden, Sterling, 31, 35, 39, 182
Heart of Darkness, 37, 51, 157
Hemingway, Ernest, 7, 24, 26, 49,
    173
Henri, Robert, 15
Henry VI, 13
Herbert, George, 23
Hercules, My Shipmate, 43
Herreshoff, Nathanael G., 53
Hills and the Sea, 163
Hitchcock, Alfred, 22
Hogg, Walter, 14
Holmes, Oliver Wendell, 134
Homer, 36
Hopkins, Gerard Manley, 100, 103
Horace, 11
Hughes, Richard, 68, 84
Hugo, Victor, 23
Human Drift, The, 45, 185

I
"Il Penseroso," 108
Innes, Hammond, 132, 164
In Hazard, 68, 84
Irish Proverb, 157

INDEX

Irving, John, 52, 59, 67, 69, 71, 87, 94, 100, 149, 166
Island, The, 185
Isle of Palms, The, 87
Italian Proverb, 34

J
Jefferson, Thomas, 19, 73
Jerome, Jerome K., 67
Johnson, Samuel, 72, 166, 179
Jones, John Paul, 54
Jones, Tristan, 69, 128, 161
Josh Billings' Wit and Humor, 142
Joyce, James, 15

K
Kazantzakis, Nikos, 151
Keats, John, 142
Keller, Helen, 173
Kennedy, John Fitzgerald, 11
Kerouac, Jack, 6
King Henry V, 51
King Richard III, 97
Kipling, Rudyard, 74, 173
Knox-Johnston, Sir Robin, 99

L
Lass That Loves a Sailor, The, 47
Leaves of Grass, 153
Lichtenberg, 100
Life of Samuel Johnson, 179
Little Women, 83

London, Jack, 45, 47, 170-171, 185
Long Day's Journey into Night, 9, 61
Longfellow, Henry Wadsworth, 24, 158
Long Way, The, 178
Loomis, Alfred F., 56
Lord Jim, 21, 149
Lovecraft, H. P., 10, 180
Lowell, James Russell, 20
Lunt, George, 25

M
Macbeth, 111
Martin, E. G., 18
Martyr, Weston, 67
Masefield, John, 55, 85, 160, 162, 175
Melville, Herman, 4, 6, 150, 158
Merchant of Venice, The, 78
Mikado, The, 45
Milligan, Spike (Terence Alan), 2
Milton, John, 22, 108
Mirror of the Sea, The, 2, 8, 10, 101, 163
Moby Dick, 4, 6, 158
Moitessier, Bernard, 93, 178
Molloy, 134
Monsarrat, Nicholas, 153
Montgomery, Roselle Mercier, 72
Morrison, Toni, 145

Mourning Becomes Electra, 15
Much Ado About Nothing, 27
"My Happiness," 137

N
Navigation of Small Yachts, The,
    143, 149
*New Universal Dictionary of the
    Marine*, 57
Nichols, Peter, 155
Nicolson, Adam, 52, 57, 83
Nietzsche, Friedrich, 137

O
Ocean Racing, 56
"Ode: Intimations on
    Immortality," 182
Odyssey, The, 36
Old Man and the Sea, The, 26, 49,
    173
Onassis, Aristotle, 143
O'Neill, Eugene, 9, 15, 61
Ono, Yoko, 166
Open Boat, The, 46, 133, 171
Othello, 77, 130
Ovid, 44, 160

P
Paine, Ralph D., 80
"Paradise Lost," 22
"Passage to India," 61
Pepys, Samuel, 84

Pericles, Prince of Tyre, 152
Pinkney, 79
Plautus, 7
Poems in Two Volumes, 5
Pope, Alexander, 146, 178
Pound, Ezra, 59
Practical Navigation, 65
Proper Yacht, The, 63

R
Ransome, Arthur, 68, 70
Redburn: His First Voyage, 150
Richard II, 90
Richardson, Samuel, 138
Rings of Saturn, The, 138
Robinson, William, 73, 182
Romeo and Juliet, 48
Rose, Robert N., 65
Rossetti, Dante Gabriel, 17
Rousmaniere, John, 76
Russell, William Clark, 90

S
Sailing Alone Around the World,
    96, 169, 175
Sailor's Proverb, 159
Sainte-Exupéry, Antoine de, 68,
    137
Salt-Water Poems and Ballads, 55
Sartre, Jean-Paul, 34
*Sea and the Wind That Blows,
    The*, 59

Sea Change: Alone Across the Atlantic in a Wooden Boat, 155
"Sea Change," 14
Sea Chantey, 41, 70
"Sea Fever," 175
Sea Is My Brother, The, 6
Seamanship, 52, 57, 83
Sebald, W. G., 138
Seller, John, 65
Seneca, 36, 143
Sexton, Anne, 6
Shakespeare, William, 2, 13, 27, 38, 44, 48, 51, 77-78, 84, 90, 97, 107, 109, 110-111, 122, 130, 152, 178
Sinclair, Arthur, 102
Singular Fate of the Brig Polly, 80
Slocum, Joshua, 27, 49, 96, 169, 175
Society and Solitude, 150
Southseaman: The Life Story of a Schooner, The, 67
Southwell, Robert, 50
Stephano, 38
Stevenson, Anne, 13
Stokes, Francis, 7, 166
"Storm, The," 92
Sunk at Sea, 80, 172
Sweet William's Farewell to Black-Eyed Susan, 46
Synge, John Millington, 19

Syrus, 163

T
Tattler, The, 169
Teaching a Stone to Talk: Expeditions and Encounters,
Tempest, The, 179
Tennyson, Alfred, 177
That Dead Men Rise Up Never, 170
"The Calm," 83, 96, 102
"The Liner, She's a Lady," 74
"The Rime of the Ancient Mariner," 11, 17, 29, 72, 76, 101, 176
"The Shipwreck," 91
"The Walrus and the Carpenter," 176
"The White Ship," 17
"The Winds of Fate," 135
Thomas, Dylan, 29, 117
Thomas, Lowell, 31
Thompson, Hunter S., 5
Three Men in a Boat, 67
Traditional Royal Navy Song, 154
Traditional Sailor's Adage, 139
Traditional Sailor's Maxim, 86, 116
Traditional Sailor's Saying,, 60
Traditional Sailor's Song, 141

Traditional Seaman's Weather
    Axiom, 114-115, 117-118, 120-
    122, 123-131
Trent, Buzzy, 108
Troup, Admiral, 144, 156
Turner, Ted, 88, 109, 150, 160,
    168
Two Years on the Alabama, 102
Typhoon, 13, 39, 101, 104-105
Thoreau, Henry David, 9, 51
Tuchman, Barbara W., 58
Twain, Mark, 167

U
Ulysses, 15
Under Milk Wood, 29
Unexpurgated Code, The, 93

V
van de Wiele, Annie, 165
*Voyages of Saint Brendan,
    The,* 16, 106

W
Wanderer, 39, 182
Ward, William A., 148
Ware, Henry, 164
*Week on the Concord and
    Merrimack Rivers, A,* 51
White, E. B., 59
Whitman, Walt, 61, 146, 148, 153

Wilcox, Ella Wheeler, 135
"Wild Nights," 32
Wilson, John, 87
Wind in the Willows, The, 77, 135
Wood, William, 79, 81, 132
Wordsworth, William, 5, 182
*Wreck of the Deutschland,
    The,* 100, 103
*Wreck of the Grosvenor,
    The,* 90
Wright, Steven, 168
Wyatt, Lorrie, 144

Y
Yachtsman's Weekend Book, The, 94
Youth, A Narrative, 64, 139, 151
10,000 Leagues Over the Sea, 182